THE BIBLE IN 10 WORDS

THE BIBLE IN 10 WORDS

UNLOCKING THE MESSAGE OF SCRIPTURE AND CONNECTING WITH GOD

DERON SPOO

Worthy
Hachette Book Group
1290 Avenue of the Americas, New York, NY 10104
worthypublishing.com
twitter.com/worthypub

First Edition: February 2020

Worthy is a division of Hachette Book Group, Inc. The Worthy name and logo are trademarks of Hachette Book Group, Inc.

The publisher is not responsible for websites (or their content) that are not owned by the publisher.

The Hachette Speakers Bureau provides a wide range of authors for speaking events. To find out more, go to www.hachettespeakersbureau.com or call (866) 376-6591.

Published in association with the literary agency of Ann Spangler & Company, 1415 Laurel Ave, SE, Grand Rapids, MI 49506.

Cover design by Matt Smartt, Smartt Guys Design.
Author Photo: Kathryn C Johnson Photography
Print book interior design by Bart Dawson.

Cataloging-in-Publication Data is on file with the Library of Congress.

ISBNs: 9781546014270 (hardcover); 9781546014911 (ebook); 9781549150470 (audiobook)

Printed in the United States of America
LSC-C
10 9 8 7 6 5 4 3 2 1

To Paula,

Twenty-five years,

One quarter of a century,

One half our lifetimes,

And it's only the beginning.

CONTENTS

ONE

A word spoken at the right time is like
gold apples in silver settings.

PROVERBS 25:11

For by your words you will be acquitted,
and by your words you will be condemned.

MATTHEW 12:37

I have a lifelong love affair with words. I am enthralled by the way words sound, what they mean, and the history they tell.

Not long ago, I was reading *The Story of English in 100 Words* by the noted linguist David Crystal. Era by era, Crystal ingeniously unpacks the English language by focusing on words as colorful as *cuckoo*, as commonplace as *street*, and as current as *twittersphere*. Crystal's brilliance is in his simplicity. He tells the story of an entire language with its history of 600 years and its 600,000 bits of vocabulary, not to mention the nuance of grammar and syntax, in 100 simple words.

Genius.

While I was marveling over the connection between the words *lord* and *loaf*, (both of which arrived in our language from the same root meaning since the head of the household was responsible for keeping the household fed), I began to wonder if it might be possible to do something similar with the language of the Bible. What if we could distill the message of Scripture, with its 750,000-plus words, into just a few that would simply but elegantly unlock its meaning? Perhaps it could be done in 100 words. Or maybe 50 or even 20 words. I didn't know. But as I pondered the possibility and began looking into it more carefully, I stumbled upon something surprising.

I knew, of course, that even as Adam and Eve fell away from God, the Lord had a plan to rescue his creation. I thought about how God had hinted at that plan in the first few pages of the Bible, as if he couldn't wait to share the good news. Then gradually, a thought began to take shape in my mind. God's plan for restoring our broken world could be crystallized in just a few words—ten precisely—all found in the first few chapters of the first book of the Bible!

When I made this realization, I was visiting South Africa. There, hosted to an evening of stargazing under the night sky, I saw the Southern Cross for the first time. This gathering of stars is not visible from my native northern sky in the United States. In much the same way, I watched words align in the first few chapters of the Bible to form a constellation I had somehow never seen before.

After jotting down my list of words from Genesis chapters 1–3, I knew it was time to embark on an exploration. I wanted to trace each word as it journeyed through Scripture so that I could more deeply understand what it would reveal about God and what he wants to say to us.

WHY WORDS?

Why this fascination with words? For one thing, it seems to me that God himself loves words.

Think about it. Genesis depicts God not as a celestial magician waving a wand over the watery void. Instead God speaks the universe into being. Light and sky, seas and stars emerge in all their swirling glory from the summoning voice of God. According to the words of Genesis:

> *Then God said,* "Let there be light," (Genesis 1:3, emphasis mine).
> *Then God said,* "Let the waters swarm with living creatures," (Genesis 1:20, emphasis mine).
> *Then God said,* "Let us make man in our image," (Genesis 1:26, emphasis mine).

Again and again, God speaks and creation spontaneously combusts into being!

Whales and wombats.

Caterpillars and carpenter ants.

Mammoths and Monument Valley.

Gravity, sea horses, supernovas, pond lilies, and the rings around Saturn.

The last on this list—Saturn's rings—is a creative feat all its own. The rings could easily wrap around twenty earths, yet they are only about thirty feet thick. Imagine, if you can, Saturn's rings represented by a DVD, with the planet itself fitting in the empty circle of the DVD center. To keep scale, the rings would be only ten atoms thick—in other words, thinner than what our eyes are able to see and what most of our minds are able to comprehend.

All of this, and so much more, is ushered into existence with words. God's creativity seems to be just that—creative. What he imagined, he made. What he conceived, he created. God's variety in creation reveals something about the vitality of his character. Our wonder-filled world comes from a wondrous God.

God created deserts as well as rain forests, and God created both to work together.

Phosphorous-rich particles of the Saharan sand, kicked up by African dust storms, are carried westward via trans-Atlantic air currents. As the sand falls earthward over South America, these particles (some 22,000 tons each year) deposit their nutrients—thus replenishing the Amazonian rain forest. Without the desert to feed the rain forest, the rain forest itself would soon become a desert.[1]

Wondrous, right?

In the beginning, God spoke for six days straight—a long run-on sentence of perfectly chosen words.

J. R. R. Tolkien wrote the famous trilogy The Lord of the Rings. While his imagination had a depth few of us could ever hope to achieve, he was a miserable typist. The story goes that he invested seventeen years of his life writing his master work. He typed every word of his manuscripts in his attic, on a manual typewriter using only two fingers.[2] Every word mattered to Tolkien! In the same way, every word spoken by God over the void-becoming-cosmos was well chosen and perfectly timed.

And then, as though verbally spent, God goes silent. God reigned content over his creation. This silence seems a bit like what we experience when absorbing the scale of the Grand Canyon or admiring the beauty of a sunset at sea. God celebrates his world with wordless reverence.

The first chapter of the Bible confirms a hunch we have had our whole lives: words have the ability to create new realities. Our words hold power. When we speak, things happen, and a few examples make the point:

- A man asks a woman to marry him. She says *yes*. The utterance of this single word unleashes a series of events that results in the creation of a new reality, something called *family*.
- A refugee finds his way to a new country. He is looking for a fresh start and better opportunities for his family. After years of filling out paperwork and taking classes, he attends a ceremony. After pronouncing an oath, he becomes a citizen. A new identity has just been forged.
- An American president—John F. Kennedy—challenged his nation to land a man on the moon and return him safely home. His words motivated the country to achieve the seemingly lofty goal in less than a decade.

Clearly, our words are powerful. By contrast, God's words are *all*-powerful. What he says is sure to happen. It's a good thing, then, that his all-powerfulness is matched by his goodness. If I had power like his, I would certainly abuse it. It would start innocently enough. I imagine instead of preparing lunch, I would simply say, "Hamburger," and my favorite meal would manifest in front of me. Rather than waking early in the morning to pour over notes and manuscripts, I would say, "Book," and my labor would be complete. On the success of such feats, my confidence and pride would grow. I would start saying phrases such as, "Six-pack abs" and "Full head of hair." Selfishness would reign. No telling what I might eventually do to someone who dare displease me. God's ultimate power is equaled by his infinite goodness. We marvel at the first. We are grateful for the second. Both know no bounds.

Fortunately, God is still speaking to us today. He communicates his power and goodness with us primarily through the pages of Scripture. The Bible is more than a single book. It's an entire library written by various authors at different points in history. Each book is the result of someone who heard God speak or saw God act so clearly and decisively that they had no choice but to write it down.

Not long ago I had the unenviable job of delivering the closing address at the end of a two-day conference. As I stood to speak, I sensed the restlessness in the room. There was no doubt everyone was ready to pack up their cars and head home. I felt certain my listeners wanted me to be done before I had even begun.

Sensing their impatience, I began with a promise. I would only give them twelve words. Of course, the twelve words would be spaced out over the span of a twenty-minute talk. But it seemed that the promise of only a dozen well-chosen words quickly eased the tension in the room. I offered three words and shared a few thoughts. I spoke the next five words and told a story or two.

Finally, I arrived at the final four words. As soon as I spoke the quartet of terms, two-thirds of the people in the auditorium began writing them down. At that moment, I knew I had won them over because most people write down what they don't want to forget.

I sometimes wonder about the people who wrote down the words of the Bible. Many of them lived in difficult times. They faced war, famine, and terrible upheavals. Like us, they must have hoped God would have stepped in and quickly resolved their problems. God's words must have been so powerful and liberating that they felt compelled to remember, commemorate, and eventually record them. The result is a book like no other book—one that provides insight on every situation or scenario life presents.

Take the book of Job for instance. Scholars believe it to be the oldest book in the Bible. The story takes place around 2000 BC, which puts it at a distance of four thousand years from us.[3] Remarkably, this ancient book still speaks profoundly about the question of suffering and God's faithfulness even in our pain. By leaning into suffering, we experience the hope-beyond-circumstance that is only found in God. Job remains as relevant today as the day it was written.

But what could the Bible have to say about more recent phenomena? What possible relevance could it have for something like the internet, for instance? Though a word search of the Bible would never turn up terms like *digital*, *online*, or *internet*, it does address issues of integrity—something sorely lacking in many people's online identity. The Bible also confronts the envy we often experience from measuring ourselves against other people's digital personas. Such comparison robs us of contentment. Scripture also speaks to our need of other people—our craving for connection that somehow goes unsatisfied despite our multitude of social media accounts. And what about Sabbath? Scripture teaches that we need to unplug from the clatter of life in order to recharge our relationship with God. Only by centering our lives in the greatest Reality of the universe—in God and his Word—can we navigate the difficult issues we face every day.

OUR FAMILY HISTORY

Though the Bible speaks to our greatest needs, it can present challenges. We wonder, for instance, what the events and people from the distant and unfamiliar past have to do with us.

As the youngest of three children, I learned many things from my older brother and sister. For instance, I learned that when they argued with my dad, they lost. I learned that when they disobeyed, they got caught, and that when they tried their hand at deception, they were found out. No matter how hard they tried to get their own way in opposition to my father, they never succeeded.

Here's a case in point. Even though both my siblings had purchased their own cars, my father had a rule. We couldn't drive to school until our senior year. For two years, they chafed at this ruling, as they grudgingly climbed aboard the school bus day after day while their cars languished by the curb. Despite their constant complaints, my father never changed his mind.

Aware that their opposition hadn't gained them anything, I chose a more subtle path. During my sophomore year, I had several appointments with an orthodontist. My dad would take time off work to drive me. After a while, I suggested it might be more convenient for me to drive myself to the appointment and then to school. I received the expected no with grace. Instead of complaining, I chose patient persistence. The next month, I asked again. And by the end of my sophomore year a yes finally came. After a month or two of solo treks to the orthodontist and school, I reasoned with my father that I had proven I could drive myself safely to school every day. Surprisingly, he agreed.

My brother and sister had taught me well. By refusing to repeat their mistakes, I experienced new freedom. (And yes, this topic of conversation is best avoided at family gatherings, but I still make sure the story is brought up at least once . . . well, maybe twice.)

What does my family story have to do with reading the Bible? Merely this: Scripture is the history of our older siblings in faith, few of whom are models of perfect obedience and holiness. Even the best of our spiritual siblings are flawed. Abraham tends to lie. Sarah abuses her maid. Jacob deceives his father. Moses kills a man and struggles with anger management for most of his life. David commits adultery and then leads a cover-up conspiracy that involves murder. Esther is hesitant. Peter plays the coward.

Many of the stories of the Bible have a cautionary edge to them. Yet these same people, seen through the long lens of time, are to be celebrated. Abraham becomes a man of faith. Sarah offers a heritage of blessing to those who learn selflessness. Jacob's character, much like his name, is changed by his brush with God. Moses delivers his people from bondage. David is remembered as a man after God's own heart. Esther risks her life to save her people. Peter is gripped by a new boldness. Whether they are good, bad, or simply clueless, we can learn much from our older siblings in faith. We bring up these stories again and again, not for how it makes these biblical brothers and sisters look, but for how their lives lend wisdom to our own.

SO, WHERE DO WE START?

Let's return to David Crystal's idea. If the story of the English language can be captured in one hundred words, why not the message of the Bible? Might it be possible to select a few words that are so significant and foundational that they provide life-giving insight into the Scripture?

This is the mission of *The Bible in 10 Words*: to help you understand God and his unstoppable love more deeply and more personally.

The words I have selected are familiar ones—as likely to come up in conversations at the grocery store, the office, or home as they are in church. Remarkably common, they are yet markedly profound.

Every day I say three simple words to my wife: *I love you.* Despite their simplicity, these three one-syllable words bear significance. My wife and I have brought three children into the world. We lost a baby. We have enjoyed long seasons of health and vacations to exotic places. But, we have also endured lengthy stints in the doctor's waiting room and late-night phone calls delivering bad news. Romance boasts its ability to climb the highest mountain, but authentic love offers to change the next diaper without being asked.

I love you.

These words can't quite capture all I want to say, all I need to say. There are times when words can fail us, refusing to capture the depth of the meaning the individual words hold. They strain under the glorious weight of our shared lives and our hope about how our future will unfold. But these three single-syllabled words I offer to Paula are all I have, so they will have to do for now.

Similarly, ten words can hardly capture the magnitude and immensity of God's love. Yet, we must work with what we have.

Each of these words communicates deeply about God and our

relationship with him and each other. Each word, found in the first page or two of the Bible, sets the stage for God's perfect world, the brokenness that follows, and the restoration God has in mind for those he loves.

LESS IS MORE

By looking at only ten words, you may wonder if I'm diminishing the value of all the other words of Scripture. On the contrary. By exploring a few words, I believe the remaining words of the Bible will come into sharper focus.

In November 1863, Abraham Lincoln stood on a famous Civil War battlefield and delivered the Gettysburg Address, a speech consisting of just ten sentences and 300 words. Immediately prior to the now famous address, a man named Edward Evertt delivered a speech that lasted for two hours. After Lincoln spoke, Evertt admitted, "I wish that I could flatter myself that I had come as near to the central idea of the occasion in two hours as you did in two minutes."[4] No doubt his listeners that day wished the same.

Instead of allowing ourselves to become intimidated by the 750,000 words of the Bible, let's narrow our focus to only ten words that explore the Scripture's central message. As we begin, let me offer a little practical advice.

This book is meant to be a pilgrimage, not a footrace. No prizes are given for finishing first. But ample treasure awaits in store for those who practice patience.

Information can be accumulated rapidly, but transformation takes time. The average person checks his or her smartphone 81,500 times each year.[5] We want to stay in touch with the office, with our family, and with the media. While many bemoan our ever-shorter attention spans, I see something more positive. Consider how life might look if we committed ourselves to keeping up with God with the same consistency we give to our devices.

Go all in! But slow down. Allow yourself to read at a leisurely but focused pace, so that you can take in what you encounter and *Who* you encounter. Marvel at the scenery and savor each step through the Scripture, so that you can experience the richness of God's Word.

Like all good things in life, this experience is better when shared. At the end of my exploration of each word, I offer a prayer worth praying and a few questions worth asking. In addition, I include three or four suggestions of other places in Scripture where this word or the idea behind it can be found. But don't be limited by my selection. Break out a concordance! Invite others to join you on the journey of relishing in ten words that will reveal a bit more of the God of the Bible.

OH, THE PLACES YOU'LL GO!

Every year, school children around the world celebrate the birthday of Theodor Geisel, better known as Dr. Seuss.

What few people realize is that in 1955, Geisel was challenged to write a book from a list of three hundred words that educators thought every first grader should know. Geisel wasn't certain it could be done until he connected two words from the list—cat and hat. *The Cat in the Hat* is 1,702 words long and uses only 220 different words.[6]

Then someone bet Geisel fifty dollars that he couldn't write a book using only fifty words. But Seuss succeeded again! *Green Eggs and Ham* uses exactly fifty different words with only one word longer than one syllable (it's the word *anywhere*).[7]

Seuss teaches us the power of well-chosen words. Quality of words is not necessarily connected to quantity. A handful of purposeful words can be profound.

The ten words that follow are deliberate. And they are intense. As you embark on these ten words, I hope you will be transformed by the deep truths contained in the Bible.

Do more than merely read these words. Experience them! Stand next to Adam in the Garden of Eden. Then sit next to Jesus in the garden of Gethsemane. Imagine yourself on the banks of the rivers running through humanity's first home, then dangle your feet in the River Jordan as Jesus wades into the water toward his destiny. Sense the depth of aloneness on the first sinner's heart as well as on the soul of the universe's only Savior. Watch Adam break into a sweat as he and Eve are caught in the first transgression; feel the sweat bead on the brow of Jesus as he pours himself out for the love of God. I pray these ten words will permit you a fresh encounter with God's love for *you* in Jesus Christ.

Listen carefully. God wants a word with you.

TALK TO GOD

Lord God,
The whole universe sprang from your lips without effort.
Tell me again about the fullness of your love.
Repeat yet again your affection in words strong and plain.

I live in loud days.
Over the noise and nonsense, I strain to hear your voice.
I am doing my best to listen.
Amen.

TALK TO ONE ANOTHER

1. Can you recall a time in your life when you sensed God was clearly speaking to you? What do you remember about the experience? What was your response?

2. Psalm 119:105 assures us that God continues to offer us guidance through the Bible. Can you recall a time when your reading of the Scripture brought clarity to a circumstance in your life?

3. How might regular reading of the Bible enrich your relationship with God? Share your thoughts.

LISTEN TO SCRIPTURE

Each of these three passages from the Bible uses the word *word*. Read each portion of Scripture aloud, followed by silence. Identify at least one benefit of listening to God when he speaks to you. I would encourage you to write down your answers in a journal.

Psalm 119:9–11
Matthew 7:24–29
James 1:22–25

TWO

Then God said, "Let there be light," and there was light.

GENESIS 1:3

I believe in Christianity as I believe that the Sun has risen, not only because I see it, but because by it I see everything else.

C. S. LEWIS, TWENTIETH-CENTURY CHRISTIAN APOLOGIST

Creation is bigger than you think. Or it may be more accurate to say that creation is bigger than you *can* think.

So far, scientists have numbered some 200 billion galaxies in the cosmos. The reality is there may be as many as ten times that number. The cosmos, it seems, is heavily populated.[1]

Creation has scale! She also holds her secrets. One hundred billion stars light up our Milky Way. Nearly the same number of neurons compose the human brain.[2] An odd coincidence, don't you think? Our neurons conspire in their choreographed chaos to make humans capable of almost infinite accomplishments. Our brains help us drive a car and drive a nail. Our brains enable us to pitch a baseball or pitch an idea to a customer. Our brains make it possible for us to read a book and to read the people in a room. How does this happen? We have our ideas, but we don't fully understand.

Creation is endless with its unexpected uniqueness.

To my eyes, all zebras look the same with their blur of black and white stripes. An African safari guide recently told me that when a female zebra gives birth, she removes herself from the herd with her newborn in tow. Alone together, the colt imprints on its mother's face. The mother's unique markings, like a personal bar code, are burned into the foal's memory. Forever after, the foal is able to recognize its mother from the markings that are unique only to her.

Here we behold the artistry of God! God was not content to

create a single zebra, which would have been feat enough. Instead God created an entire species with each individual zebra given a face-sized fingerprint to distinguish its identity. In addition, he gave the foal its ability to remember and recognize its mother as a result of the mother's God-given impulse to be alone with her young. Identity. Ability. Instinct. And this is only the zebra! Such mind-boggling uniqueness repeats itself throughout all of God's creation. Creation is both majestic and mysterious.

LET THERE BE LIGHT . . . AND LAWS

God inaugurates the universe with a simple command: "Let there be light." The cosmos is born! The very word *cosmos* helps us appreciate the role of the universe. Coined by the Greeks, *cosmos* was a word used to describe the ornaments on a woman's clothing. Ornaments, we all know, add beauty to an object of value. We still tip our hat to the origin of this word when we refer to cosmetics which serve to ornament a person's beauty.[3]

As I write these words, it is nearing Christmas. Each year, we put up the tree in our family room. Then we break out the ornaments. The entire family participates. Each member of our family has an ornament that is special to us. We adorn the tree, making it more beautiful with something we value. Seen this way, the cosmos is an ornament enhancing the already-beautiful character of God. Creation adds to the beauty of God's goodness and power to those who choose to see it.

With the words "Let there be light" (Genesis 1:3), God issues the first command of his universe-building opus. Photons leapt from the lips of God, and for the first time light sped across space at its signature velocity.

I am convinced something more than visible light is created here.

The sun, moon, and stars—the objects connected with physical light—do not make their appearance until the fourth day. So what else is happening?

I venture that from the very beginning, God laid down the foundational laws that govern our universe. The laws of physics are put in place. Likewise, the spiritual foundations of all creation are established. Just as gravity is important and must be observed, so too God puts the spiritual laws in place that we ignore at our own peril.

These spiritual realities are not difficult to see.

First, the universe is good. God follows the declaration of "Light!" with the exclamation, "Excellent!" At its essence, the universe is a good place created by a loving God. Take God's word for it—the world is a gift.

The Bible takes exception to the belief—both ancient and modern—that the world is inherently evil. Many early cultures had their own stories to explain the world's beginnings, and typically these accounts require an adult rating for violence.

The Mesopotamian's *Enuma Elish* serves as a good example.[4] The god Marduk defeats the deity Tiamat. In triumphal rage, he cuts her corpse in two. With half he makes the sky, and from what's left he forms the ocean. The Mesopotamians saw the world as a violent place. Who could blame them? Their experience with nature, its storms and lightning and wind, and their contact with outside people, the invaders and marauders and captors, convinced them the world is out to tear people apart. That's how it started, and that's how it is.

But Genesis sees the cosmos as ornamental to God's character. Perhaps how God formed the world and what we have made of it are two different things. His good gift to us is meant to be enjoyed. The Hebrew word for "light" is used exactly seven times in Genesis 1. To the modern mind, seven is little more than a prime number. But to the ancient Hebrew mind, seven was a God-number—the primary number used to represent divinity. Thus, God's sevenfold proclamation of goodness is equivalent to the Eternal's ultimate seal of approval. The Bible's first chapter reminds us creation is a good gift from a good God. Life is not to just be endured, but enjoyed. Smell the fresh coffee. Taste the medium-well fillet. Relish the touch of your lover's hand. Run your fingers through your toddler's curly locks of hair. Stop overlooking. Cease the taking for granted. Savor. Appreciate.

A second essential foundation is the uniqueness of God. Here again, the ancient mind imagined a universe crowded with deities. Each god offered specific perks as they wielded their slice of power. One god might grant good crops while another was able to ensure a house full of children. Genesis 1 turns us toward a simple reality: only one God inhabits heaven, and only one God blesses the beings of earth. Other pretenders to the throne are just that—pretenders.

Theology offers a word for the uniqueness of God—monotheism. How unromantic! I prefer to say that God is unique. He is the uncreated Creator. The unnameable Namer. God alone is unlimited, unrestrained, uninhibited, and unstoppable. Only he is invincible, incomparable, irrepressible, and inconceivable. A lone voice spoke existence *into* existence. Even now, only one voice is worthy of our rapt attention and total affection.

When God physically stepped into his creation, he sacrificed many things, but not his uniqueness. John Stott, a leading voice among twentieth-century Christians, offers this:

> For he [Jesus] is unique in his incarnation (the one and only God-man), unique in his atonement (only he died for the

> sins of the world), and unique in his resurrection (only he has conquered death). And since in no other person but Jesus of Nazareth did God first become human (in his birth), then bear our sins (in his death), and then triumph over death (in his resurrection), he is uniquely competent to save sinners.

In short, Stott concludes, Jesus is not "the Great," he is "the Only."[5]

A final spiritual foundation of our universe is—and this is a bit more subtle than the others—the patience of God.

Being a full-on type-A personality, I like to get things done. For a day to be successful, a certain number of items must be removed from my list and taken off my mind. For the most part, my method serves me well. But one disadvantage plagues me: in the rush of doing, I neglect the simple joy of being.

Just this week, I sat on my front porch reading a book. My daughter, home from university, took a seat next to me for a talk. We spoke about boys, God, work, worry, and the always-approaching future after college. During our conversation, I was secretly fighting the voice in my head begging me to return to my book to conquer my quota of pages for the day. If I am not careful, my need for accomplishment will rob me of the joy of such intimate moments.

Once God created light—both physical and spiritual—his ever-expanding to-do list was set aside. God called it a day! He relished the light. Like a child content to dance in the rain, God bathed in the bright beams of his creation. God enjoyed the moment. Time, now that it existed, could wait. If this is how God appreciates light, might this tell us something of his affection for us? I am certain it does.

God is patient. Even as we ignore him for many long years, he is patient. His stamina exceeds our stubbornness. He does not nervously tap his toe. He extends his steady and open hand always further as he awaits our homecoming.

OUT LIKE A LIGHT

Absolute darkness is unsettling. Add to that that I was only ten years old and ninety feet underground. My family was visiting the Sonora Caverns of far west Texas. It is odd to imagine that there are watery caves below the dry desert surface. God's mysterious and majestic creation knows no bounds. Our tour guide explained stalactites and stalagmites. While rushing water erodes rock, dripping water forms rock. Each slow-moving drop of water deposits its minerals. Over the course of centuries, caves are transformed into subterranean cathedrals.

I was fascinated until our guide turned out the lights. The complete darkness unnerved me. My father was standing beside me, and as the darkness gripped my young frame, I instinctively took a step closer to him. He was already near me, but I wanted *nearer*.

Have you noticed how we instinctively use the language of darkness to describe life's difficulties? Think of history. World War II with its Nazis and atomic bombs and concentration camps is called a "dark chapter" from our past.

We use darkness to describe evil actions. Abusive parents are discovered to live just down the street. A school shooting takes place in our town. Suddenly, we realize that these dark events are no respecter of persons or personal space.

We even use the language of light and dark to describe our emotions. When life is good, we exclaim, "The future looks bright." I have a naturally buoyant disposition, but years ago I sank into an unexplainable and seemingly inescapable depression. I still refer to it as my "dark time." I, like many Jesus-followers before me, felt the words of the psalm writer when he prayed, "Darkness is my only friend," (Psalm 88:18).

Perhaps you have seen the horror movie where a hapless character hears a strange noise in the basement. We want to tell her to stay in the safety of the well-lit room. Instead, she insists upon descending the dark, creaky stairs in search of the bump in the night.

That's the feeling I get when I read Genesis 3. Adam and Eve are safe in the light of God's clear commands. Their curiosity cracks open the door of disobedience with nothing but darkness behind it. The pair descends the shaky stairs of their own impulsive desires. With each step they made an excuse. *Did God really say no? Doesn't it look good for food? We want wisdom, don't we?* Finally, the door at the top of the staircase slams shut behind them. Total darkness. God presented Adam and Eve with a plain choice: *Stay in the light or step into darkness.* Genesis memorializes their choice, and we inherited a world darkened by sin.

Like my younger self in the cavern, so we find ourselves in darkness today. Adam and Eve's disobedience to God darkened not only the world but also their hearts. Darkness is around us. Darkness also finds its way inside us. We all have made the choice to live outside God's light.

Oceanographers have a name for the deepest reaches of the ocean. Anything below twenty thousand feet is labeled the hadal zone—in honor of the mythic Greek god Hades (fittingly, a name synonymous with hell). The pressure of such depths is hard to fathom. Imagine one hundred elephants standing on every inch of your body and you get the idea. The crushing depth is paired with total darkness. Light from the sun does not penetrate this part of the ocean.[6]

Isn't this an accurate picture of the way life typically feels? Extreme pressure. Excessive darkness. We grit our teeth under the weight of life's burden. We grope our way from one difficult circumstance to the next. People pressure us. Circumstances confuse us. Is this how life must be? Is this the best we can hope for? Are we doomed to crave the light but to endure nothing but darkness? Is Adam and Eve's heritage our only inheritance?

LIGHT AT THE END OF THE TUNNEL

What most people commonly call the Old Testament, I prefer to call the Older Testament. *Old* implies obsolete, while *older* connotes greater longevity and more experience. (My brother would rather I call him *older*, not *old*. See the difference?) As a prime example of this, the Older Testament lends us its legacy and expertise by offering consistent pleas and prayers for light:

- "The LORD is my light and my salvation—whom should I fear?" (Psalm 27:1).
- "For you rescued me from death, even my feet from stumbling, to walk before God in the light of life," (Psalm 56:13).
- "LORD, you are my lamp; the LORD illuminates my darkness," (2 Samuel 22:29).
- "Your word is a lamp for my feet and a light on my path," (Psalm 119:105).

I remember being amused the first time I read Psalm 119:105 in a paraphrase of the Scripture called *The Living Bible*. The translation reads, "Your words are a flashlight to light the path ahead of me." This modern twist on ancient words sounds silly at first, but I would have welcomed even the smallest flashlight in the cavern encounter of my childhood.

We long for light. It is for this reason that the arrival of Jesus is best pictured as a bright eruption in a dull and darkened world. A new day, likened only to the first day of creation, has dawned!

"The people who live in darkness have seen a great light, and for those living in the land of the shadow of death, a light has dawned," (Matthew 4:16). God's creation is given a second opportunity to embrace light. Adam and Eve had the choice—to stay in the light or step into darkness. Now our choice is like theirs only reversed: to stay in the darkness or be led into the light.

John, the Gospel writer, speaks of Jesus's arrival with these words: "In him was life, and that life was the light of men. That light shines in the darkness, and yet the darkness did not overcome it," (John 1:4–5).

Scholars seem to be torn by meaning of the word *overcome*. John chooses a Greek word that means "to grasp." The confusion comes from the multiple meanings of this word in the Greek language. The English language is really no different. We can grasp an idea with our mind. We may also grasp our enemy by the throat. Grasping implies either the effort to understand or the attempt to overpower.[7] But does it have to be one or the other? Can't it be both?

And yet the darkness did not grasp it. Do we stay in the darkness of ignorance or be led into the light of truth?

A fourth-century Christian named Gregory of Nyssa said, "If a man in broad daylight freely chooses to shut his eyes, it is not the sun's fault when he fails to see."[8] Jesus taught and healed. He performed miracles and spoke to the meaning of life in plain terms. Yet, the prevailing religious opinion toward Jesus was one of rejection. They refused to understand him. It still happens today. Many screw their eyes shut, unwilling to grasp that Jesus is God's light for a dark world.

And yet the darkness did not grasp it. Do we stay in the darkness of hatred toward God or be led into the light of love?

The political machinery of Jesus's day did its best to destroy and dispose of Jesus. Jesus himself referred to the moment of his arrest as an hour of darkness (Luke 22:53). Darkness hung him out to dry, but darkness could not hold him down. Jesus pulled free from death's dark grip.

Many still reject Jesus to this day. Many still hate him. Passive-aggressives and aggressive-aggressives in their disbelief and disgust toward God still persist in darkness. Yet Jesus still illuminates. "I am the light of the world. Anyone who follows me will never walk in the darkness but will have the light of life," (John 8:12).

And yet the darkness did not grasp it. On more than one occasion, I have imagined my life without the light of Jesus. Surrounding this imagined outcome of my life without Jesus is an overarching sense of darkness. Indeed, each of us must address our own eternity-making moment: we can stay in the darkness or be led into the light.

THE LEGACY OF LIGHT

So, what does this mean to live in the light? The Apostle Paul gives us a clear idea, "For you were once in darkness, but now you are light in the Lord. Live as children of the light—for the fruit of the light consists of all goodness, righteousness, and truth," (Ephesians 5:8–9).

Children of light. An apt metaphor! Children are naturals. Not content with sitting, they push on to standing, walking, running, riding a bike, driving a car, and leaving home. Not one of these accomplishments is easy at first. But as soon as they master one feat, they move to the next. The way Paul sees it, to be adopted as God's child is to embrace a lifestyle of change. And the specific areas of growth? Paul lists three.

Goodness

Children of the light decide to be good for the world. As God labeled the light of Genesis 1 "good," so the children of light live to benefit wherever in the world God chooses to place us. I have long taught that Christians ought to be the easiest people on the planet with which to get along. I wish this were true. Dallas Willard issues this challenge: "Churches should do seminars on how to bless and not curse others."[9]

Are you looking for a life of greater adventure? Practice a simple habit: Bless every person God puts in your path. Your spouse, the person who hands you your dry cleaning, the security guard at the office, the waiter at the restaurant, the unreasonable parent at the sporting event—share with them what God has shined on you.

The same Jesus who says *to* us, "I am the light of the world," (John 8:12; 9:5) says *of* us, "You are the light of the world," (Matthew 5:14). We reflect the light—the goodness of God—which we have been granted.

Righteousness

This high-sounding word is not as difficult as it appears. Notice only the first five letters. R-I-G-H-T. Righteousness is a relationship put right. Righteousness is a relationship at complete peace.

Thomas Merton says, "We are not at peace with others because we are not at peace with ourselves. And we are not a peace with ourselves because we are not at peace with God."[10] Merton is right—we lack rightness in our relationships. The remedy begins with God. The resulting inner peace can't help but permeate outward into every relationship we have.

I have a neighbor who doesn't care for me. If I am honest, it is tempting to hate him in return. But this is the path of least resistance. God calls me to right relationship. As Jesus-followers, we treat others no longer based on what we think they deserve, but based on how God directs us. Our treatment of others does not depend on our opinions but on obedience to the one we call Lord. The Apostle John sums it up this way: "Anyone who claims to be in the light but hates his brother or sister is still in the darkness," (1 John 2:9, NIV).

Truth

William Barclay, one of the great commentators on Scripture, says, "There are two revelations in Christianity; there is the revelation of God and the revelation of ourselves. No man ever really sees himself until he sees himself in the presence of Christ."[11]

No longer need we guess about God. Jesus is his ever-living embodiment. Everything that is true about Jesus is true about God.

Is God a healer? Certainly. We see Jesus healing eyes and ears and tongues and making what was blind, deaf, and mute to see and hear and speak.

Is God patient? Definitely. Jesus is not easily upset by sinners. In fact, he seems quite at home around people who own their brokenness. It is only those who pretend to be perfect who test the patience of Christ. Says Richard Rohr, "Holier-than-thou people usually end up holier than nobody."[12]

Is God living? Absolutely! Jesus's walk out of the grave is a reminder to every person of all ages that God is stronger than death's intimidation.

If all this were not enough, we also have the immense joy of discovering the truth about ourselves. Never again do we need wonder or worry about our true worth. We are not alive by chance. Nor did Jesus offer himself for us by accident. We are not alone in the universe, and the light of every new day reminds us that God can be trusted with life's overwhelming choices and mundane minutia (Psalm 143:8).

Jesus himself challenged us to serve as a light in our world (Matthew 5:14–16). Paul's words in Ephesians help us understand what Jesus meant. We shine with goodness toward others, with a passion for relating rightly to God, and with a commitment to truth wherever truth leads us.

A DIFFERENT LIGHT

The Bible ends as it begins—with light. Light existed before the advent of sun, moon, or stars. Likewise, long after our sun exhausts its energy and the moon's orbit decays and all the stars go supernova, light will still exist. Life, which began in a garden, will find its final home in a city. This new city, however, will be unlike any city we know from experience. No overcrowding. No crime. No stench of refuse. No buzz of neon or harsh glow of incandescence.

Heaven, it seems, will not need what we now know as "natural light."

> The city does not need the sun or the moon to shine on it, because the glory of God illuminates it, and its lamp is the Lamb.
>
> —Revelation 21:23

> Night will be no more; people will not need the light of a lamp or the light of the sun, because the Lord God will give them light, and they will reign forever and ever.
>
> —Revelation 22:5

As in the beginning, so for eternity—light! God, infinite in goodness, plain with truth, and the one who makes all relationships right will finally and fully be ours to enjoy! We will bask in the glow of his glory.

It is hard to imagine what we will see in this new light. Perhaps the closest we can come to imagining is thanks to Don McPherson. McPherson set out to offer better protection to the eyes of doctors who perform surgeries using powerful lasers. McPherson developed Enchroma, a substance that filters out certain damaging levels of light.[13] But, unintentionally, McPherson's Enchroma made it possible for other wavelengths of light to be seen in new ways. For the first time, color-blind people using McPherson's glasses are able to see the reds and greens that for so long have eluded them. It is worth taking the time to watch the tearful family videos of people experiencing the full spectrum of color for the first time. They didn't know what they were missing. In their first moment behind their new lenses, the wearers are overwhelmed by color more beautiful than they had imagined.

Will it be so for us when we finally and forever step into the full light of God? I believe so. We will see everything clearly for the first time. Perhaps we will wonder how we missed the beauty that was in front of us all along. The full spectrum of God's goodness and truth and righteousness will be as plain as the first day. And it may take all of eternity for our eyes to fully adjust.

TALK TO GOD

Lord God,
You are complete goodness, absolute truth, and real righteousness.
More than these words define you, you define them!
Shine yourself again on my gray and sin-shadowed soul.

My world—much like my heart—is dark and damaged.
I long to see the uncreated light
Of your perfect Presence.
Amen.

TALK TO ONE ANOTHER

1. What is your favorite experience with light—sunrise, candlelight, porch light—and how does your experience of its goodness remind you of God?

2. Think about the role light plays in creation. Why do you think "being light" is an appropriate metaphor for what Christians should be in the world?

3. Identify a few people you know who because of their goodness, truth, and righteousness model what it means to be a child of the light.

LISTEN TO SCRIPTURE

Exodus 13:21–22

Psalm 27:1–3

Matthew 5:14–16

1 John 1:5–7

THREE

The Second Word
DUST

Then the LORD God formed the man
out of the dust from the ground.

GENESIS 2:7

All we are is dust in the wind.

KERRY LIVGREN, LEAD SINGER OF
1970S PROGRESSIVE ROCK BAND *KANSAS*

We are barely beyond the Bible's first chapter when we are faced with the uncomfortable truth that we come from dust. Behold our unsophisticated beginnings!

Genesis 1 tells us what we *want* to hear: We are more like God than anything else in all creation. God's image inhabits our identity. DNA and divinity coalesce to create our humanity.

Genesis 2, however, tells us what we *need* to hear. We are brought back down to earth by revealing that we are made, not from precious elements like silver or gold or even useful alloys like bronze or copper, but from mere dirt—the stuff that clings to our boots and settles on our furniture, the tiny particles that can be brushed off with a feather duster.

Modern science bears this out. Ninety-nine percent of the human body is composed of five basic elements: carbon, hydrogen, nitrogen, calcium, and phosphorus. Nothing special at all. We find these same elements in the charcoal in our grills, the laundry detergent in our utility rooms, and the toothpaste by the bathroom sink.

We are commonplace. But the knowledge of our substance is more than a chemistry lesson. The earthiness of our identity is a hidden gift. Our grittiness is an expression of God's good grace.

JUST-DUST-NESS

Our just-dust-ness informs us that we are frail.

Frailty greeted me this morning as I pulled myself out of bed. I enjoy getting up an hour before everyone else in my family. The house is quiet, and I enjoy the solitude and productivity of the early morning. But the action of getting up is difficult! Most mornings I feel like the disciples in the garden of Gethsemane on the night of Jesus's arrest. I sense his voice inviting me to join him in the day, but I hear my body demand just a few more moments under the comforter. My spirit is eager but my body aches. Indeed, most moments provide some reminder of frailty. It may be a hungry stomach or a thirsty throat. Feet ache. Eyes burn. Muscles spasm. Tighten and tone your body as you please, but you will never escape frailty's easy reach.

A behind-the-scenes look at the New York City Marathon more than makes the case. Organizers distribute no less than 62,000 gallons of water, 42,000 energy bars, 32,000 gallons of Gatorade, over 13,000 bandages, and 390 tubs of petroleum jelly.[1] (Runners know chaffing is no laughing matter.) The participants are well trained and finely trimmed athletes. But remove hydration and nutrition for but a short time and the marathon would surely lead some to the morgue. Even at our best we are still frail.

We bruise. We get fevers. Our heads hurt. We become arthritic. Joints wear out. Skin wrinkles. Follicles die. And ultimately we atrophy. And the finish line of our frailty is a thing called death.

But weren't Adam and Eve originally created to be immortal? That's certainly what my Sunday school teacher taught me. But the truth is humanity was mortal from the beginning. A naturally immortal being would not need access to the tree of life that Adam and Eve required. Physically, humanity has always been finite. From the beginning, our life has been dependent on God's generosity.

Paul Kalanithi spent a large part of his life training to be a neurosurgeon. Just as he was reaching the top of his field, he received a diagnosis—cancer. His prognosis turned terminal. With the little time he had left, Kalanithi penned a memoir of mortality:

> I began to realize that coming in such close contact with my own mortality changed both nothing and everything. Before my cancer was diagnosed, I knew that someday I would die, but I didn't know when. After the diagnosis, I knew that someday I would die, but I didn't know when. But now I knew it acutely. The problem wasn't really a scientific one. The fact of death is unsettling. Yet there is no other way to live.[2]

Frailty.

Mortality.

Just dust.

Why does God reveal that we come from dust? What could we possibly gain from such knowledge? What does our frailty teach us other than we are sure to die?

First, our just-dust-ness is a tangible reminder of God's intimate involvement in our lives. He "formed" the first person from the dirt of the earth (Genesis 2:7). The picture is of an artist shaping pottery. God did not slop us together. He sculpted us (Isaiah 64:8).

The work of a potter at the wheel is both messy and physically demanding. Spatters and sore muscles result along with the beauty of a handmade creation. So, too, God sinks his hands into the soft loam of earth to form Adam. Even now, God doesn't hesitate to dig his fingers into the messiness of our lives. He doesn't mind getting his hands dirty. He wants to be intimately involved.

Psalm 103 celebrates the qualities of God's intimate nature. Each line of this poem-turned-prayer gives us greater and greater confidence in God's involvement in our lives. God's love is higher than the span between earth and sky. God's affection throws our sin beyond the farthest horizon. Like a father with his beloved child, so God gives us more chances than we deserve. Yet even as this psalm celebrates God's greatness, we are sobered by our smallness:

> For he knows what we are made of,
> remembering that we are dust.
> —Psalm 103:14

God keeps our composition clear in his mind. Of all the things God would think about us, why this?

This brings us to the second benefit of our just-dust-ness: humility. The very word *humble* finds its roots in the earth—from the Latin *humus*, another word for "the ground." [3] God has given us the gift of groundedness. Pride, says the Bible, is self-destructive (Proverbs 16:5 and James 4:6). Thinking too much *of* ourselves, and thinking too much *about* ourselves, leads only further and further away from God. Staying grounded keeps us close to our Creator.

Not long ago, I published my first book. The experience was heady, complete with press releases, television interviews, radio talk shows, book signings, and speaking engagements. One day I ventured into a local bookstore with a single goal in mind: I wanted to see my book on the shelf. When I couldn't find it, I asked for help.

"We sold out of that title," the attendant told me.

"Really? That's great to hear. You see, I'm the author," I said while trying to mask my thrill. I instantly imagined a long line of people vying for the last copy on the shelf like people fighting for the latest model smartphone.

"Yes," continued the clerk, "we had only one copy in stock. And since it sold, we haven't gotten around to ordering another one."

I heard the almost-audible thump of my ego as it fell back to earth. Once again I was grounded. Simply put, I needed the reminder of why I wrote the book in the first place. My motivation was not sales, but souls. Certainly a book can be both a bestseller and a life-changer. But, at least for me, the first feeds my pride while the second cultivates a bit more humility.

Humility is seeing ourselves accurately. It's what allows us to relate to God as our Creator and Sustainer, helping us remember that we are created beings who require constant care.

God is indispensable; I am expendable. God is eternal; I am just passing through. He is deity; I am dust.

But does the truth of our fleeting existence diminish our worth?

Beauty is temporary. Indeed, it is beauty's impermanence that adds exquisiteness. Plastic flowers may be pretty, but they are not beautiful. In contrast, consider the bloom of blue bonnets. For six weeks each spring, these unpretentious plants paint their blues across the desert and hills of my native Texas. No sooner do they bloom than they die. But their brevity only adds to their beauty. Their fleeting fragility and mortality deepen our appreciation for their present moment of splendor. Didn't Jesus say the same thing? "Observe how the wildflowers of the field grow: They don't labor or spin thread. Yet I tell you that not even Solomon in all his splendor was adorned like one of these. If that's how God clothes the grass of the field, which is here today and thrown into the furnace tomorrow, won't he do much more for you—you of little faith?" (Matthew 6:28–30).

The momentary and the magnificent meet!

As with flowers, so with the folks God created. We are magnificent!

In the hands of God, common molecules become masterpieces. The "average person" is composed of 60 trillion cells, 7 billion capillaries, 5 million hairs, and 3 million sweat glands.[4] If our physicality is this breathtaking, then can you imagine the majesty of our unseeable parts? Far from ordinary, our intricate details bear the fingerprints of our eternal Creator.

Temporary? Certainly.

But beautiful? Absolutely.

Our just-dust-ness gives life an urgent edge. The noted writer Philip Yancy was in a near-fatal car accident. As he lingered between life and death, he found himself pondering a few basic questions: "*Who do I love? Who will I miss? How have I spent my life? Am I ready for what's next?*"[5] Profound questions. And I see no reason to wait until the moment of death to ask them. Time is short, and we dare not put off such matters for another day.

THE DIRTY DEED

Dust testifies to our creation. Dust also bears witness to the curse now clinging to our souls.

Michelangelo's *Pieta* is among my favorite sculptures. A grieving Mary cradles the crucified Christ. For five hundred years, this sculpture has captured Mary's love for her son and her poignant sorrow—the grief known only to parents who have lost a child. Decades ago, a man leapt over the altar railing and began hammering the figure of Mary—damaging her face and left arm. What required the master's chisel months to create took a madman's hammer only moments to destroy. While the damage was repaired, the sculpture now sits behind glass, adding both a layer of protection and greater distance for the eyes longing to appreciate the artist's work. Now we all pay for one person's failure of self-control.[6]

Satan handed Adam and Eve the hammer, but they were the ones who decided to wield it. By choosing self-will over God's will, they ignored God's clear instructions in order to indulge their curiosity and desires, resulting in their own destruction. Like the *Pieta*, we now all pay the price for Adam's indiscretion. God spelled out the consequence in poetry:

> You will eat bread by the sweat of your brow
> until you return to the ground,
> since you were taken from it.
> For you are dust,
> and you will return to dust.
> —Genesis 3:19

Theologians traditionally refer to this moment as "the fall." In the beginning, human beings must have been magnificent, the pinnacle of God's creative genius. It is accurate to say that Adam and Eve broke the commands of the Lord. But it is also true to say that they broke themselves against God's clear commands.

And what remained? Only shattered fragments of their former selves. Just dust.

Some physicists calculate a speck of dust is halfway between the size of a molecule and the size of earth. Hard to imagine, isn't it? We are composed of dust yet capable of infinite potential. Intimacy with God unlocks our greatness. Selfishness only diminishes our worth. Eternity could have been ours! Our choices lead to our erosion.

This original disobedience has consequences for us all. Humanity has been crumbling ever since. As descendants of Adam and Eve, we, too, are destined to decompose. Someday in a cemetery, your family and friends will leave your body in a box and drive off to enjoy a meal.

While they feast to your memory, you will begin the silent but sure process of returning to the basic elements from which you came. Dust is your destiny.

The Tomb of the Unknowns in Arlington National Cemetery holds the remains of one unidentified soldier from every American conflict since the First World War. Within the tomb, the casket of the soldier from World War I rests on a two-inch layer of French soil. The soil of battle was the scene of his demise. It is odd to think that the battlefield and the battler are made from the same substance—just dust.

One day soon, all our battles will be done, and we, too, will be laid to rest. Those who remember us will also die. Ultimately, we will all be forgotten by our world. We will become unknown, and all our dreams will be dust.

Does this sound gruesome? Does this feel hopeless? It is.

The Artist's work was vandalized. Our stature, like Michelangelo's statue, was smashed. Instead of being whole, we are fragmented. Instead of bearing only the chisel marks of our Creator, we now bear the hammer scars of our own failure to trust the goodness of God and rightness of his commands. We are crumbling. Ultimately we will die and disintegrate completely. God would be entirely within his rights to sweep us under some corner of creation's rug as nothing more than a failed experiment of love. Fortunately, he has no intention of forgetting us.

DOING THE DIRTY WORK

The Apostle Paul, reflecting on the opening scenes of Genesis, wrote these words:

> The first man Adam became a living being; the last Adam became a life-giving spirit.

> The first man was from the earth, a man of dust; the second man is from heaven. *Like the man of dust, so are those who are of the dust; like the man of heaven, so are those who are of heaven.* And just as we have borne the image of the man of dust, we will also bear the image of the man of heaven.
>
> —1 Corinthians 15:45, 47–49, emphasis mine

Paul is clear. You and I did not make the conscious decision to be born. We are descendants of Adam by no choice of our own. By contrast, the spiritual life made available by Christ becomes ours only if we choose it. We didn't ask to be made like Adam—just dust. But only we can decide to walk through the door of immortality opened wide by the resurrection of Jesus. Jesus did the dirty work of dying and defeating death on our behalf. Physical life and death are beyond our control; spiritual life and the offer of an eternity that follows stem from a decision that is entirely ours to make.

The fate that awaits those who reject this Christ-given opportunity of immortality is a discussion for another time. For now, let's consider three grand realities experienced by those who choose to move beyond dust into an unstoppable existence.

First, *God is the giver of life.* This is a basic truth. But how essential!

God does not love us because *we* are good; he loves us because *he* is good. And his goodness overflows in the act of granting us a life that outlasts our physical existence. As an encore to our Genesis 2 origin from dust, God scoops up what is left of our former selves. Between his fingers we are formed yet again, only this time into something that will never erode, decay, or decompose.

An oft-repeated story tells of a minister visiting the home of a woman whose rent was past due. He had come from church with enough money to cover her payment. Though he knocked on her door, no one answered. Later, she confessed she had ignored his knock because she thought it was her landlord coming to collect the rent rather than a friend coming to pay the rent.

Such a misunderstanding—to mistake a giver for a taker.

As God knocks on the door of our lives, our first instinct is to suspect that he is out to take something from us. Our fun or freedom, perhaps. Or maybe he will take away our hopes and dreams. We suspect he will rob us of something we cherish, when in fact he wants to restore all that we lost in the fall thousands of years ago—our true identity.

If this is so, why must we still face physical death? Here is the second great truth: *Death is transformed from something inevitable into something hopeful.*

A date waits for you and me on the calendar. As the day of our birth sits behind us, so the day of our death stands in front of us. It waits for our arrival, and it refuses to be moved. But this date is the very doorway to our destiny.

If we belong to Christ, our physical death is only the final step—albeit a difficult one—toward our ultimate destination. When we take our final breath, the experience that will follow will leave us breathless. If we fear dying alone, we may now lay that fear to rest.

Not long ago, I was visiting a pastor who's also a good friend. As we were talking, the telephone rang. It was an out-of-state call informing us that a mutual friend by the name of Paul had died. Oddly enough, Paul had been the one who had introduced us years earlier. What were the odds that the two of us would be together when the news arrived? For a long moment we sat in silence, aware of the gift Paul had been to both of us. That moment of silence was also a gift because we knew Paul's life, far from being over, was only just beginning.

Know this: At the moment you step through death's dark door, you will be met by the face of a friend. Jesus himself will help you release your final breath, enabling you to take your first steps into a larger life. Your final frail gasp will be met with his firm grasp as he holds your life in hands scarred by his sacrifice for you.

Remember, too, that he won't be asking you to do anything he hasn't already done. In fact, he was the pioneer who first charted the terrain between the valley of our current existence and the highlands of immortality (Hebrews 12:2). Because of him, we will experience more than life *after* death; we will experience life *instead* of death.

And this hope fuels a third powerful promise: *We will be completely restored.*

Will we meet with a physical death? Certainly. But physical death becomes a doorway to the larger life beyond, a momentary inconvenience as we step into a fuller existence. And as we cross this threshold, every bit of care and curse will be dropped at the door.

Helen Keller, who went blind before the age of two, put it well: "Death is no more than passing from one room into another. But there's a difference for me, you know. Because in that other room I shall be able to see."[7]

Are you battered? You will be healed. Burned out? You will be born anew. Impaired? You will be impervious to weakness. Nothing about you will be less than perfect. And your restoration will transcend the physical. Mentally, spiritually, emotionally, psychologically you will be whole. Every trace of sin will be erased. The journey of life is hard with its bumps, bruises, and tragedies. But you will soon know a day when you will be fully restored and finally at home.

In my role as a pastor, I stand over many gravesides. My practice for years has been to read the words of Paul from another part of

1 Corinthians 15: "For this corruptible body must be clothed with incorruptibility, and this mortal body must be clothed with immortality," (1 Corinthians 15:53). I don't understand all that this means. But somehow God will take the raw material of our physical bodies and transform them into something new and indestructible. Like the resurrected body of Jesus, our own resurrected body will have moved beyond the reach of illness, pain, disfigurement, and death. We will no longer be just dust. We will be eternally immortal.

A saint from centuries past, named Irenaeus, offers that Christians share so fully in God's gift of life that "they will forget to die."[8] A powerful thought! Perhaps you have experienced something similar when you forgot to eat because of work on an important project or you forgot to go to bed because you were enthralled by a movie. What does heaven hold for us? We won't be able to take our mind off God and his lavish gift of life. And death? It will never cross our mind. And our amnesia will render us immortal.

We once were merely descendants of Adam. Now we have become more. We are dependents of Jesus Christ. In this life we know grit. The next life will hold only grace.

SHAKING THE DUST FROM OUR FEET FOR THE FINAL TIME

In Christianity's early days, the Roman Empire considered Jesus-followers a threat to national security. One Christian, a gardener named Phocas, used his crops to feed the poor. He found himself on Rome's most-wanted list. One day, as Phocas worked his small patch of earth, he encountered soldiers who had been dispatched to kill him.

Inquiring where they could find him, he replied, "Yes, I know Phocas well. But it is late in the day. Come inside. Rest. Let me prepare a meal for you. In the morning, I will take you to Phocas."

From his meager means, Phocas prepared the meal. He gave the soldiers the most comfortable sleeping arrangements. As they slept, Phocas slipped into his garden and dug a grave. The next morning, after serving the soldiers breakfast, Phocas broke the news.

"I am the man you are looking for. I am Phocas."

The soldiers were stunned. Had this been a trap? Had they been poisoned? No. Phocas explained that he had lived a full life, and he was prepared to meet his final fate. The soldiers struggled with the thought of murdering a man who had shown them only hospitality. But Phocas convinced them that they had a duty to perform and perform it they must.

"I have one request," Phocas said. "Bury me in my garden."

So the soldiers did. Discharging their duty, they dispatched this Christian man toward eternity.[9]

If we are just dust, this story makes no sense. In fact, it is tragic. If all the existence we ever taste is only in this life, then we had better gulp down every mouthful we can manage. But if we are more than dust, then Phocas's story ends very differently. In fact, it does not end at all.

And your story, in Christ, ends-yet-begins the same way.

Longfellow's simple words serve as the final word of our destiny:

Life is real! Life is earnest!
And the grave is not its goal.
Dust though art, to dust returnest,
Was not spoken of the soul.[10]

TALK TO GOD

Lord God,
My body is borrowed earth. My worth is in the fingers that formed me.
You made me once. Make me again into something new.
Keep me still as you finish your work.

I am but a speck, yet so much more.
In you, I am light and I am salt.
I am your child infinitely loved.
Amen.

TALK TO ONE ANOTHER

1. Why do you think God wants us to understand our just-dust-ness? Describe how your knowledge of the brevity of life does or doesn't shape the way you live.

2. Psalm 103 says God remembers that we are dust. What do you think that means? How is it comforting to know God remembers us as dust?

3. Is it beneficial for Christians to ponder the reality of death? How does Jesus and his resurrection change how we think of our mortality?

LISTEN TO SCRIPTURE

Job 10:8–12

Job 34:10–15

Psalm 90:1–6

Ecclesiastes 3:19–22

FOUR

Then the LORD God formed the man out of the dust from the ground and breathed the breath of life into his nostrils, and the man became a living being.

GENESIS 2:7

Don't try to explain it, just bow your head // Breathe In, Breathe Out, Move On

JIMMY BUFFETT, AMERICAN MUSICIAN AND SONGWRITER

Patty Ris was enjoying her lunch in the dining hall of her senior adult community center when she began choking on a bite of food. Another resident, noticing Ris's distress, sprang into action. He wrapped his arms around her and delivered several sharp compressions just below her rib cage. The Heimlich maneuver he performed saved her life. Her rescuer was none other than ninety-six-year-old Dr. Henry Heimlich. While his signature technique has saved countless lives, he himself had never performed the maneuver in a real-life emergency.[1]

Breath is life! We are able to live weeks without food and days without water, but without air, we expire in a matter of minutes. Every minute our bodies require about four gallons of air while resting, six gallons while walking, and twelve gallons while running. During our lifetime, we will take in some seventy-five million gallons of air.

As a young father, my habit was to check on my children in the middle of the night. I trained my ear to hear the gentle sound of their breathing. Just to be sure, I would place my hand on their small stomachs until I felt the rhythmic rise and fall of respiration telling me all was well.

Genesis 1 tells the true story of God forming and filling creation. What God formed in the first three days, he filled in the latter three. He formed light, sea, and earth on days one, two, and three. Then on days four, five, and six, God filled the sky with celestial bodies, the sea with creatures both majestic and miniscule, and the earth with flora, fauna, mammals, and marsupials.

God created the first human in much the same way. He formed Adam from the ordinary elements of the earth. But Adam was not yet alive. He had skin and sinew, but no spirit. Only when God filled Adam with his own precious breath did Adam join the ranks of the living. God's breath birthed in Adam the rhythmic pulse of life.

It is no accident then that the words for *spirit* and *breath* are the same in the Hebrew tongue. *Ruach* represents both the spirit in our body and the breath in our mouth. The Greek language follows suit. *Pneuma* (think pneumonia) means both spirit and breath. God gave humans the gift of breath.[2] The invisible parts of our humanity were created at this mysterious moment. Air filled Adam's lungs. Now a spirit also inhabited his body.

Some ancient creation accounts provide a jarring contrast to this beautiful scene of gifted life. In one Mesopotamian epic, gods were murdered and their tears and blood and flesh were used to create humanity.[3] In other words, death was necessary to generate life. How different is the Hebrew picture! *Life* bestows life. God himself provides the spark that ignites the flame of our existence. One of Job's well-meaning but ill-timed friends was right when he said, "The Spirit of God has made me, and the breath of the Almighty gives me life," (Job 33:4).

And what God gives, he also has the right to take away. Job's friend was correct yet again when he pronounced, "If he put his mind to it and withdrew the spirit and breath he gave, every living thing would perish together and mankind would return to the dust," (Job 34:14–15).

TAKE MY BREATH AWAY

Sin's ultimate consequence is that it severs us from our life-giving relationship with God. Death is our lot. Psalm 104 reminds all who will listen of this truth. Speaking to God, the psalmist says, "When you hide your face, they are terrified; when you take away their breath, they die and return to the dust," (Psalm 104:29).

In the final hours of life, many people begin a labored form of breathing called the "death rattle." I have heard it many times on my visits to the palliative care ward of the hospital. At life's end, breathing becomes work. The death rattle sounds so uncomfortable that a person's final breath feels like a gift. The battle to breathe is over. The body may finally rest.

"Death rattle" is not a phrase appropriate for polite company. The Bible offers friendlier expressions. The book of Genesis chooses a euphemism that is both picturesque and polite. Of Abraham it says, "He breathed his last," (Genesis 25:8, NIV). The same is said of Ishmael (Genesis 25:17, NIV), Isaac (Genesis 35:29, NIV), and Jacob (Genesis 49:33, NIV). Genesis, in fact, is the only Older Testament book to use this idiom. The same writer who portrays God as the giver of breath makes it clear that this gift comes with an expiration date. (The very word *expiration* means "to breathe out"[4] or, to put another way, to run out of breath.) Like it or not, peacefully or painfully, we will all run out of breath and die.

Louis Armstrong grew up on the rough-and-tumble streets of New Orleans. Early on, he learned how to make money by making music on street corners. To keep his money from being stolen, he carried his coins in his mouth. This, along with his unique style of playing his trumpet, earned him the name "Satchelmouth," which was later shorted to "Satchmo." Armstrong and his band recorded more than sixty records. His most famous song was "What a Wonderful World," recorded in 1967. His graveled and gritty voice encourages us to pause and ponder the gift of life in all its ordinary splendor.[5]

The breath Satchmo breathed so successfully into his trumpet finally ran out in 1971. The world went on being wonderful, but Armstrong no longer enjoys it. The music plays on, but Satchmo no longer hears it. This is the lot of all people—artist and plain folk alike. The death rattle will one day choke out our ability to regale and relish life. A hopeless thought. Yet, it is reality.

But might death itself, as depressing as it is, hold some small benefit? Is God powerful enough to transform the curse of death into some kind of blessing? Of course! Two such benefits come to mind.

First, not knowing the timing of our death, we learn to rely on God for such matters. Ecclesiastes 3:2 reminds us there is "a time to give birth and a time to die." We have little say in the timing of birth and death, so we learn to trust God with both.

Second, our days being limited, we treasure whatever time we are given. I regularly hear the saying, "The days are long but the years are short." With age, I now see the wisdom concealed within this cliché.

Another way of grasping life's brevity is what I call "the toilet paper spool" philosophy of existence. I admit this is a less-than-charming idea. The spool at the center of a fresh roll of toilet paper turns slowly at first, given the large circumference of tissue. But as the roll is depleted, the cardboard center turns ever faster. The roll reaches its top speed as the last square of the paper is pulled.

The similarity between the ignoble toilet paper roll and the noble life God has given us is striking. At first, life seems to move slowly. I remember it felt like an eternity until I became old enough to drive. My years in college and graduate school felt like time standing still. I experienced what felt like decades of time in the few calendrical months between my engagement and marriage.

Now, however, life seems to spin ever faster. It was only yesterday that my children were in diapers tucked safely in bed. Now they are in cars driving across the country. I remember agreeing to serve my church as their pastor. Almost instantly, twenty years have come and gone. Life, like the spool of toilet paper, continues to pick up speed. Soon the last day will jolt and life as I know it will jar to a stop. It makes me appreciate every hour, day, season, and moment a bit more.

Michael Casey writes, "In some monasteries the church door leading to the cemetery was inscribed with the words *Ille hodie et ego cras*. Today he; tomorrow me."[6] As indispensable as I might feel to the events of today, should I die, the world will hardly note my absence. The psalmist teaches us to pray this way: "You return mankind to the dust, saying, 'Return, descendants of Adam.' For in your sight a thousand years are like yesterday that passes by, like a few hours of the night," (Psalm 90:3–4).

SAVING YOUR BREATH

Earlier, I stated that Genesis is the only book in the Older Testament to use the expression "breathed his last." It would be the only book in the entire Bible were it not for two New Testament writers who resurrect the phrase. The Genesis idiom is used in the New Testament for none other than Jesus himself and the most important death of history.

Mark says, "Jesus let out a loud cry and *breathed his last*. Then the curtain of the temple was torn in two from top to bottom," (Mark 15:37–38, emphasis mine). Luke's record of the same moment says, "And Jesus called out with a loud voice, 'Father, into your hands I entrust my spirit.' Saying this, he *breathed his last*. When the centurion saw what happened, he began to glorify God, saying, 'This man really was righteous!'" (Luke 23:46–47, emphasis mine).

Both accounts have something in common. What appeared at first to be a final ending was, in fact, a new beginning. Jesus's final breath created an opening in what previously had been closed.

In Mark's telling, the focus is on the most holy place in the temple where God was believed to dwell. For long centuries this area was sealed off by a large curtain keeping ordinary people on the outside looking in. But with Jesus's final breath, a gaping hole was cut in the curtain. Like an adventurer trekking through the jungle cutting a swath of new trail, Jesus's final breath cut the temple's curtain in half, permitting us to follow him into the presence of God. But Jesus will not force this restored relationship with God upon us.

While Mark is fixed on a Jewish curtain, Luke focuses his attention on a Roman centurion. Something happens within this soldier's heart as he realizes he had witnessed the crucifixion of a man whose identity was far more than a common criminal. *This man is righteous* is the soldier's single-handed reversal of the lower courts' decisions. Let the Jewish religion and the Roman institution condemn Christ; this soldier would choose admiration instead.

Open temple. Open heart. Jesus's last breath creates new possibilities and decisions we never knew existed. The temple curtain is open. The matter of an open heart is what each of us must decide for ourselves.

I have several good friends who are morticians. Privately they have confided to me that as they embalm a human body or dress it for viewing, they speak to it. They explain to the corpse what they are doing and why they are doing it. My mortician friends tell me this is a simple way of giving dignity to the deceased. For some, I am sure it is also a coping mechanism to relieve the stress from the gruesome but necessary task.

After Jesus's final breath, he, too, was dressed and buried. I wonder if Nicodemus and Joseph of Arimathea spoke to the lifeless, breathless body of Jesus. As they anointed him with spices and wrapped his body in strips of linen, what, if anything, did they say? No record of such one-sided conversations exist, if they happened at all. If they did, Jesus could not have spoken for himself. He was dead, and his spirit was elsewhere.

But if the duet of undertakers had listened carefully, they would have heard more than they could comprehend concerning this young Messiah. His last breath had opened temples and hearts. Split them, in fact. A way was available. To believe was an option. But the grief of the moment made them deaf to the new reality of an opened-wide restoration with God.

A powerful last breath! One that still echoes into the ear of our human longing and lostness. He had breathed his last. Or had he?

BREATHE NEW LIFE

In C. S. Lewis's classic children's book *The Lion, the Witch and the Wardrobe*, Lewis lends his imagination to the resurrection of Jesus. Lewis describes Narnia as a land where it is "always winter and never Christmas." The White Witch, the Satan-figure of the story, holds the land in a forever-frozen state. Worse, she has changed a few unfortunate creatures into stone statues to decorate the entrance of her icy castle. Aslan the Lion, representing the risen Christ, having defeated death, leaps boldly into the witch's courtyard.

> "Hush," said Susan, "Aslan's doing something."
>
> He was indeed. He had bounded up to the stone lion and breathed on him. Then without waiting a moment he whisked round—almost as if he had been a cat chasing its

> tail—and breathed also on the stone dwarf, which (as you remember) was standing a few feet from the lion with his back to it. Then he pounced on a tall stone Dryad which stood beyond the dwarf, turned rapidly aside to deal with a stone rabbit on the right, and rushed on to two centaurs.[7]

Aslan, in his life-giving escapade, alters the landscape of the witch's courtyard. At the crescendo of the scene, Lewis writes, "Everywhere the statues were coming to life. The courtyard looked no longer like a museum; it looked more like a zoo."[8]

Lewis's fanciful retelling captures the real-life power of Jesus's resurrection. The disciples must have feared for their own lives now that Jesus was dead. Would the Jews be out for them next? Would the Romans identify them as co-conspirators in a revolt? Even the missing body of Jesus and rumors of resurrection was not enough to thaw their hearts and limber their rigor-mortised minds.

As it turns out, the disciples had nothing to fear from an imagined sting operation of the Jews or the ruling Romans. Instead, it is Jesus who pounces upon them. Without warning, he is in the room. The doors are locked, yet Jesus is miraculously present. "Jesus said to them again, 'Peace be with you. As the Father has sent me, I also send you.' After saying this, he breathed on them and said, 'Receive the Holy Spirit,'" (John 20:21–22).

Jesus breathed on his disciples—fresh air into their frozen forms. Just as God had breathed life into an empty Adam, Jesus breathed new strength into his dumbfounded disciples. Like Aslan among the witch's statues, followers were reborn. And this new fresh breath was not only for this small group. Jesus offers to breathe on a world of souls too long shut off from the life-giving God.

At a time of year called Pentecost, the Holy Spirit was sent by God. Just as Lewis pictured dwarfs and dryads and centaurs, so the disciples witnessed "Parthians, Medes, Elamites; those who live in Mesopotamia, in Judea and Cappadocia, Pontus and Asia, Phrygia and Pamphylia, Egypt and the parts of Libya near Cyrene; visitors from Rome (both Jews and converts)" breathing in a new life (Acts 2:9–10). Acts 2 is still happening today. Filipinos, Ecuadoreans, Iranians, Indians, Native Americans, Aboriginals, and Haitians are among the variety of individuals on display as changed people.

The effects of this are personal. The God who *formed* you now *fills* you. You are emboldened to exchange your predictable plans for the uncharted adventures God has in store for you. Your destiny is his to decide. His Spirit fills you with a confidence not your own, and he deflates any thoughts of personal inadequacy. His Spirit empowers you to resist sin's powerful pull and endows you to experience unanticipated levels of holiness.

A simple chorus, while a bit dated, offers a perfect prayer for God's fresh filling.

Breathe on me. Breathe on me.
Holy Spirit, breathe on me.
Take thou my heart. Cleanse every part.
Holy Spirit, breathe on me.[9]

On a corporate level, breath forms and fills the church—a group of people that transcends every man-made category. Jew and Gentile, rich and poor, men and women, ancient and modern all identify with each other though the life of Christ more than we do through our race, status, gender, or era.

I have spent the greater part of twenty years trying to breathe life into the gasping group of folks called the church. The natural drift of a church is toward institutionalization—becoming a museum or, worse, a mausoleum. Once young and brash, I am now more seasoned and humbled. The fresh breath of life is not mine to give. Only Jesus can transform museums into zoos. For this, I will wait and work and hope and pray. Occasionally, I see signs. I feel the church's chest rise and fall with the new promise of life.

Recently, our church experienced a rash of illnesses. Difficult pregnancies, cancer diagnoses, and extended hospital stays overpopulated our prayer list. We set aside one Sunday to invite people to our altar for anointing with oil. The Scripture is plain about such matters: "Is anyone among you sick? He should call for the elders of the church, and they are to pray over him, anointing him with oil in the name of the Lord," (James 5:14). After sharing this scripture with the church, I admitted anointing with oil for healing is not a particularly "Baptist thing," but I assured my church that it is the biblical thing to do. I held aloft a vial of oil I had purchased on a recent pilgrimage to the Holy Land. I explained that I had procured it from one of Israel's most sacred sites—Ben Gurion Airport near Tel Aviv. My point? The oil was a product of the Holy Land, but it was purchased in an ordinary place. Likewise, a holy God is not indifferent to our pedestrian needs. The oil itself contains no magic. It is a symbol of God's power to heal. I was concerned if my sometimes-staunch church would respond to the invitation. But like oil, the people flowed into the aisles and spilled themselves upon the altar. It was a profound and beautiful time.

Several weeks later, a woman reported to me that her doctor had reversed a diagnosis that would have required surgery and an extended recovery. Do I have the gift of healing? No. But God does, and always has. How I love serving in the zoo of the church! Zoo animals can certainly make a mess. But the power of this life makes it worth the momentary untidiness. The church is filled with living examples of the love of God which has captured us, yet at the same time sets us free.

DON'T WASTE YOUR BREATH

Teddy Roosevelt was a sickly child. The robust man we picture as our twenty-sixth president began as a frail boy who could barely breathe. The young Roosevelt suffered from acute asthma. On the nights when the attacks were their worst, Roosevelt's father would carry young Teddy around the house until his breath returned.

> If this ritual proved inadequate, he would call for the servants to bring the horse and carriage round. Wrapping the gasping child in a blanket, he would drive the horse at a good clip through the gas-lit streets, believing that the bracing night winds would stir the child's lungs. "Nobody seemed to think I would live," Roosevelt later recalled. "My father—he got me breath, he got me lungs, strength—life."[10]

Jesus breathes new life and strength into our gasping frames. And for what reason? What do we do with this new gift of breath, lungs, strength—life? It's not complicated, really. We use our new God-given breath to bless others and praise God.

Bless Others

Blessing is a spiritually tinged way of saying that we benefit the lives of people around us in the way Jesus would if he were in our place. The infinite opportunities! How might our attitude toward the day transform if we embrace every interaction with others as an occasion to better their lives? We begin, of course, with our family. Respecting our spouse and encouraging our children is a privilege. Instead of neglecting them, we treasure them. We give them the best of ourselves, not whatever might be left of us at the end of the day.

As we move into the larger world, we see opportunities to act in ways some may consider unconventional but are in step with the Spirit's work. Instead of cursing, we bless. Instead of talking harshly, we make eye contact and speak with respect. Instead of considering what to extract from every person we meet, we mull over how we might sacrifice for the very people God loves. Most of all, the deepest need of every person we meet is Jesus Christ himself. To communicate his love in plain and profound ways is the ultimate and eternal way of blessing others.

My old mentor, Calvin Miller, signed his letters with "100,000 Blessings—Calvin." How audacious to believe we might exponentially bless those around us. However, if we have indeed inhaled the Holy Spirit into our lives, the supernatural becomes the most natural way to live.

Praise

Breath's highest honor is to be used in worship of the giver of all good things—both his grand graces and his little kindnesses.

G. K. Chesterton put it like this:

You say grace before meals.
All right.
But I say grace before the play and the opera,
And grace before the concert and pantomime,
And grace before I open a book,

And grace before sketching, painting,
Swimming, fencing, boxing, walking, playing, dancing;
And grace before I dip the pen in ink.[11]

A fitting way for a follower of Jesus to live! Why spend our breath grumbling? Worship is the highest use of breath. Complaining is its most tragic waste. No wonder Paul commanded, "Do everything without grumbling and arguing, so that you may be blameless and pure, children of God who are faultless in a crooked and perverted generation, among whom you shine like stars in the world . . ." (Philippians 2:14–15). Christians should be the most positive people on the planet! Followers of Jesus stand apart and stand out by the way we bless God with every breath he has given us.

The book of Psalms culminates with this kind of worship. After all the mourning and moaning and pleading and pursuing of God, Psalm 150 puts the previous one hundred forty nine psalms in perspective.

Hallelujah!
Praise God in his sanctuary.
Praise him in his mighty expanse.
Praise him for his powerful acts;
praise him for his abundant greatness.

Praise him with trumpet blast;
praise him with harp and lyre.
Praise him with tambourine and dance;
praise him with strings and flute.
Praise him with resounding cymbals;
praise him with clashing cymbals.

Let everything that breathes praise the Lord.
Hallelujah!
—Psalm 150:1–6

Worship is using our borrowed breath for its highest possible purpose. Worship is returning our breath to its rightful owner—an act of grateful surrender that should permeate every part of our existence.

TALK TO GOD

Lord God,
You exhaled into Adam and he inhaled life. I need the same!
But I inhabit a sin-smogged, care-choked world.
Please, don't hold your breath! And don't hold it back from me!

Resurrected, Breathing Christ,
Infuse life into my gasping frame.
Resuscitate. Rejuvenate. Resurrect.
Amen.

TALK TO ONE ANOTHER

1. What can we learn from God's design of us as "breathing" creatures? Have you experienced a time when you had trouble breathing?

2. How is our breath (our experience of God's good gift of life) affected by sin and a fallen world? Sometimes we have

trouble breathing physically. Have you ever experienced something similar spiritually? Have you ever felt spiritually strangled?

3. Jesus describes the Holy Spirit as a wind (same word for breath), and he "breathes" the Holy Spirit on his disciples. What can we learn about the Holy Spirit from Jesus's use of this metaphor?

LISTEN TO SCRIPTURE

Job 34:14–15
Ezekiel 37:1–14
Acts 17:22–25

FIVE

The Lord God planted a garden in Eden, in the east,
and there he placed the man he had formed.

GENESIS 2:8

We all long for Eden, and we are constantly glimpsing it: our whole nature at its best and least corrupted, its gentlest and most humane, is still soaked with the sense of "exile."

J. R. R. TOLKIEN, TWENTIETH-CENTURY AUTHOR,
BEST KNOWN FOR THE LORD OF THE RINGS TRILOGY

God certainly knows how to pay a compliment.

God knows quality when he sees it. God's mind reverberates with the chorus "It was good" seven times in Genesis 1. On the seventh occasion, God improvises his mental refrain with "It was very good." This is no mere pleasantry. Creation bears its Creator's seal of approval.

One creature stands out with distinction—humanity. Adam and Eve are more like God than anything else God created, and God placed his prized people in a special place, a place unlike anywhere known before or since.

When my wife and I began our courtship, I wanted every outing to be memorable, but my funds were limited. The finer restaurants were out of my financial reach. But what I lacked in cash, I compensated for in creativity. On one occasion, I deputized a friend to go ahead of us to the local burger joint and prepare a table for our date—white table cloth, fine china, and silverware were borrowed for the occasion. We dined in luxury that evening. The food was the typical fare, but in our minds we were five-starring it. Other customers stared. No matter. My future wife understood. In fact, she still mentions that date even now. Why? She understood my desire to create something special for her.

God shows the same care toward his first creation. But unlike my past self, God has unlimited resources. From his infinite wealth of love, God created the perfect environment for his prized creation. God made a garden.

The garden, we are told, was in the east. In ancient parlance, *east* describes more than a physical location. *East* also meant "early"—fitting, given that the sun rises from that direction. "In the east" is the ancient author's way of saying, "A long time ago in a garden far, far away."

THE SECRET GARDEN

A garden? Is this really the best God can do? To understand Genesis 2 fully, we must push aside our modern notions of flora and fauna. Pansies and petunias this was not. To the ancient mind, a garden was special for two reasons: what it contained and who lived next door.

The Contents

The White House, 10 Downing Street, and the Kremlin are modern descendants of a time-honored tradition. Rulers have a special place of residence. In the ancient world, a king reigned from his palace. Next to the palace, the king owned a personal garden. These gardens were to display the great variety of life found in the king's realm. Animals and plants from the far reaches of the kingdom reminded the king and his visitors of his vast power.

Remember Daniel? It was his habit to pray three times a day facing his faraway home of Jerusalem, first as a lowly captive of the Babylonians and later as a senior adviser to Persian royalty. Even when the Persian king made it illegal to do so, Daniel prayed on. As punishment, he was thrown into the lion enclosure. Daniel 6 spells out Daniel's miraculous survival. One may wonder why the king had a lions' den in the first place. The Persian dictator was keeping an already ancient practice. Lions had been imported to bear witness to his expansive territory. And if the lions provided a convenient form of execution, all the better.

In a way, the king's garden was a microcosm of his realm. As a creative way to ponder this idea, think about Florida. Florida's history is littered with invasions of the worst the world has to offer.

Over the years, owners of pythons and boa constrictors in Florida, tired of their omnivorous pets, have released them into the wild. An alien environment typically proves too much for lesser snakes. But pythons and boas know how to dominate their adopted ecosystem.

A traveling circus in the early 1920s accounts for Florida's armadillo problem. A half dozen or so of these resilient animals escaped their enclosures and the population boom began!

As if this weren't enough, the melaleuca tree was imported from Australia as a natural means to drain swampland. Only too late did Floridians learn that melaleuca trees spread at an alarming rate and are nearly impossible to kill.

The list goes on—fire ants, meat-eating piranhas, and a breed of toad with a sting containing a powerful and painful toxin—all dumped on Florida.

The irony? Ponce de León, the famed Spanish explorer, gave Florida its name. *La Florida* is Spanish meaning "place of flowers." Ponce de León imagined Florida a garden paradise. Unfortunately, it has become something far different.[1]

Florida illustrates Eden-in-opposite. Florida contains the worst, Eden the best. Florida's environment has become hostile to its inhabitants. Eden was the ideal environment. Florida is an easy target. Eden was a place of protection.

Adam and Eve's presence in the garden is proof of the place humanity holds in the heart of God. And even better than what the garden contained was who happened to live next door.

The Neighbor

We were created to spend our lives close to God. It's really that simple. This is what God originally intended for each of us. God wants to be close to those he loves the most.

Perhaps no one has explored this neighboring with God in the Garden of Eden more thoroughly than a scholar named John Walton. Walton helps our modern mind wrap itself around the ancient understanding of Eden. The Garden, he says, "is [God's] place for residence, it is a place for relationship. . . . It is also a place for his rule."[2]

Residence.

Relationship.

Rule.

This is paradise! Residence—Eden is where God called home. Relationship—of all the neighbors God could have, he chose us. Rule—God wanted Adam and Eve to know more than regulations; he wanted them to know him. Eden was a place close to the throne and heart of God.

So, why would anyone risk throwing all this away?

LED DOWN THE GARDEN PATH

Intimacy with God and proximity to his presence comes with clear expectations.

> The LORD God took the man and placed him in the garden of Eden to work it and watch over it. And the LORD God commanded the man, "You are free to eat from any tree of the garden, but you must not eat from the tree of the knowledge of good and evil, for on the day you eat from it, you will certainly die."
>
> —Genesis 2:15–17

When I read this passage, my eye is drawn to the word *free*. "You are *free* to eat." An odd idea to embed into a restriction, don't you think? This is the first time, but by no means the last, Scripture challenges our commonly held concept of freedom. We are tempted to think of freedom as indulging our every impulse without any restrictions placed upon behavior. *This is real freedom!* we tell ourselves.

What we discover, often too late, is that this brand of freedom isn't free at all. If we embrace this faux freedom, we will eventually find ourselves held hostage by the very habits we once controlled. We call this addiction—enslaved by the very thing we once considered freedom. I have many friends who once viewed the bottle as the epitome of liberty. But soon alcohol became their unshakable idol. Sex promises to be the great liberator, but soon free love becomes a tormentor demanding more and more to keep satisfied. A friend from my early years told me quitting drugs was far easier than giving up smoking. But what once looked cool proved to be a merciless captor.

Self-control is our natural immunity against behaviors or habits that are self-destructive. But the disease of addiction attacks and destroys our God-given self-defenses. Addiction is something we convince ourselves we can control until we have no other choice but to admit that it now controls us.

Notice the first freedom of Genesis 2. It is the die from which all freedoms from God are cast. Authentic freedom is always accompanied by some form of restriction. But how can this be true freedom? Perhaps a picture will help.

My son recently completed his final season of high school baseball. Caleb's love for the game began with the agonizing experience of T-ball. I do not personally hold to the Roman Catholic belief in purgatory, but after sitting through a season of preschool-aged T-ball, I was forced to rethink my position. Purgatory, if it does exist, shares a great deal in common with a T-ball doubleheader.

Through the years, my son progressed through coach-pitch baseball on to kid-pitch games then into the quiet years of junior varsity. Finally, Caleb emerged on the varsity squad. One rule remains true in baseball regardless if it is the T-ball or the varsity variety: for the hit to count, the ball must fall within the white-chalked lines that fan out from home plate. Any hit that lands outside these lines is foul and the hitter tries again.

But you might protest, *That's not right! Why enforce arbitrary boundaries on a well-intentioned batter? Each hitter should decide for themselves what is fair and what is foul!*

I suppose the game could be played with no agreed-upon boundaries, but such a game would quickly become unbearable to watch. I can imagine fielders traipsing through the parking lot and bleachers for a ball that before would have been foul while the hitter jogs at a victor's pace around the bases. With each player determining for themselves what is fair or foul the game would degenerate into chaos.

Seen this way, the foul lines are key to enjoying the game of baseball. Every batter is *free* to hit the ball anywhere within fair territory. The possibilities are endless: lay down a sacrifice bunt to move a runner into scoring position, drive a ball over the head of the shortstop in a well-executed hit-and-run, or win it all with a walk-off homer. The constraints are the containers of freedom.

The Creator invited Adam and Eve to a life of joy and intimacy. Freedom is found within the boundaries of his clear commands. But another voice competes for the first human's attention—that of Satan. "This is not freedom," he challenges. "How dare God tell you how to live your life. What gives him the right? You are missing out! If you want it, take it. Seize the fruit! *Carpe Fructus*!"

At stake in Genesis 3 is a fundamental decision we all face in life. The choice is this: Am I willing to accept right and wrong, based not on what I feel, but based on what God reveals? Will I trust my instincts or God's instructions? Will I draw on my experiences—limited though they are—or God's commands regardless if they make sense to me in the moment?

"Don't eat from one specific tree" is hard to misinterpret. So too is "Do not commit adultery." Yet our desires disagree. *One dalliance won't hurt, will it? Haven't I been a good boy all these years? No one understands me like she does.* Suddenly, the crunch of forbidden fruit is between our teeth, and we are surprised when it turns bitter. This is but one example among many. We could say the same about truth and lies, stealing and generosity, or truth telling and gossip mongering.

Worldview is a sophisticated way of saying "the way I see life." At the epicenter of how we see the world is the discernment of good and bad, right and wrong, the acceptable and the best. Who we give the final say to in such matters determines who will be the ultimate authority over our lives.

In the end, Eve and Adam found themselves expelled from the Garden. Theirs was an exile of their own making. If Adam and Eve were bent on living life without God, then God would honor their wish. God created people for closeness. Estrangement was a consequence of their shortsighted choice.

GARDEN VARIETY

Jesus had a fondness for gardens.

Some of his stories were set in gardens (Matthew 7:15–20). Jesus used the role of a gardener as an example of God's care for his people

(John 15:1–2). Ironically, Jesus was once mistaken for a gardener (John 20:15).

Jesus also had a favorite garden. During the final week of his earthly life, he repeatedly retreated to a special garden overlooking Jerusalem. Stress was taking its toll, and Jesus found solace there. Even though Judas failed to understand Jesus's mission, Judas knew Jesus well enough to know where to lead the arresting party.

> He [Jesus] went out with his disciples across the Kidron Valley, where there was a garden, and he and his disciples went into it.
>
> —John 18:1

The garden of Gethsemane still receives visitors today. Gethsemane means "olive press." True to its name, Gethsemane is filled with olive trees. In Jesus's day, the olives were processed on site—pressed until they surrendered the last drop of their useful oil.

On my first visit to Gethsemane, I was astonished to learn many of the olive trees in the garden today were already alive when Jesus visited. My amazement fed my imagination. *Perhaps Jesus knelt near this tree when it was but a sapling. Did this tree overhear the words of Jesus to his disciples and to his Father?*

Jesus's choice of a garden on the eve of his arrest was no mere coincidence. Jesus used every means available to teach his followers. Throughout his ministry, he used words. On the evening of his arrest, around the Passover table, Jesus used the symbols of bread and cup. Now, in Gethsemane, it was Jesus's actions that lent instruction. Did the disciples immediately make the connection between Eden and Gethsemane? Maybe not. But as they replayed and relived the scenes leading to their master's crucifixion, they no doubt marveled at what they had missed in the heat of the moment. Eden and Gethsemane illustrate humanity at its worst and best.

Adam and Eve said to God, "Not your will but ours." Jesus said to the Father, "Not my will but yours."

The duo in Eden chose defiance. The one in Gethsemane chose surrender.

Adam and Eve took a fruit that did not belong to them. Jesus gave his life, something he had every right to keep.

Eden was the natural habitat for obedience, yet Adam and Eve chose rebellion to God. Gethsemane was a hostile environment of stress and doubt, yet Jesus chose full obedience to God's will.

Eden, a place of perfection, produced the world's first sinner. Gethsemane, imperfect though it was, played host to the world's only Savior.

Adam and Eve were expelled from Eden against their will; Jesus, arrested in the garden, went without resistance.

Adam and Eve disobeyed because they felt God's commands were unfair. Jesus obeyed even when the justice of God didn't make sense.

Adam and Eve fed their own urges; Jesus hungered only for God.

And Gethsemane isn't the only garden to appear at the end of Jesus's earthly life. Throughout his final hours, gardens continue to make their cameos. One such garden is called Golgotha.

> There was a garden in the place where he was crucified. A new tomb was in the garden; no one had yet been place in it. They placed Jesus there . . .
>
> —John 19:41–42

The tempting tree of Eden promised life but delivered death.

Golgotha's tree pointed to death, yet it has become our ultimate source of life.

As if Gethsemane and Golgotha were not enough to drive home the reversal of Eden, the first rumbles of resurrection were also felt in a garden. There, a band of women found something they did not expect. There, too, a pair of disciples saw what they could not explain.

Remember the purpose of the king's garden? Gardens exhibit the best that a kingdom has to offer. Jesus's journey through the gardens puts God's power on full display. In Gethsemane he surrendered to God. At Golgotha, he sacrificed his life. And in the garden tomb he won victory over death. Indeed, God's best!

I BEG YOUR PARDON; I NEVER PROMISED YOU A ROSE GARDEN

The language of gardens and gardeners crops up time and again in the New Testament. American theologian Victor Kuligin, who has spent his life teaching in Africa, offers this: "The New Testament borrows liberally from the language of agriculture to speak about the life of a believer. Sow, plant, reap, harvest, prune, water, and grow are consistently used in this way."[3]

Galatians 5 is the epitome of the garden metaphor: "But the fruit of the Spirit is love, joy, peace, patience, kindness, goodness, faithfulness, gentleness, and self-control," (Galatians 5:22–23). God intends our character, like a well-planned and well-planted garden, to be fruitful.

Over the years, I have discovered for myself the joy of gardening. Horseradish and peppers are my favorite crops. In fact, an unspoken competition exists among pepper gardeners for the hottest produce. Plant breed, soil composition, and rainfall amounts all play a part in contributing to the pain of the pepper when it finally touches the tongue.

My friend, Luis, tells me of his Rodriguez family lore. The pepper's heat is directly tied to the emotional state of the person who planted the jalapeños. An unbearably hot pepper is blessed with the benediction, "Mama must have been angry when she planted these!"

My point is this: gardeners take pride in their produce. Galatians 5 reveals that God feels the same way. What does God want? Fruitful character! Great and noble deeds have their place, but God prefers character over charisma. Mother Teresa put it like this: "We can do no great things, only small things with great love." The same idea can be used for each of the Galatian fruit.

We can do no great things, only small things with great joy.

We can do no great things, only small things with great kindness.

We can do no great things, only small things with great self-control.

You get the idea.

How do we develop these character qualities? The short answer is we can't.

Note the label on the produce. Galatians does not call it the fruit of the *Christian*. They are branded as the fruit of the *Spirit*.

We are Eden, and God himself is our Gardener.

Jesus said, "I am the true vine, and my Father is the gardener. Every branch in me that does not produce fruit he removes, and he prunes every branch that produces fruit so that it will produce more fruit," (John 15:1–2). Our participation in the process of fruitfulness is to remain connected to Christ, our vine. God is the one who makes growth happen in the Christ-follower's character.

A gardener must do more than merely hope for a good crop. Action is required to ensure he gets the harvest he wants. So how does a gardener act like a gardener?

As Jesus already mentioned, a gardener must have the nerve to prune his plants. If we didn't know better, we would think the gardener is wounding the plant when in fact he is making future fruitfulness possible. God, sheers in hand, removes every unfruitful part of life—uncontrollable sins, unbeneficial relationships, or unnecessary habits or attachments. Whoever coined the phrase "the first cut is the deepest" never experienced the pruning touch of our gardener-God. Every cut, it seems, is deeper than the one before as God removes everything un-Christlike from our character.

God also weeds our lives. God is intent on removing from our surroundings anything that confines or crowds our growth (Matthew 13:41; Mark 4:7).

God does not plant us in isolation. We are not alone in his garden. The Bible pictures the church as a crop from which God expects a bumper harvest (James 5:7).

A gardener must also be a keen-eyed guard. A gardener assumes the role of protector from any force that might threaten to invade and harm his garden. Enemies come in all shapes and sizes—from ants to birds to rabbits. Size is irrelevant. If it means to destroy, a diligent gardener declares war (Matthew 13:41).

Might God also fertilize? Yes! He is a generous gardener. At God's disposal are riches beyond our ability to fully appreciate. Life-giving relationships and life-changing circumstances push our roots ever deeper into the rich soil of the Spirit.

In Christ, you and I are God's garden. Eden is still alive! The best of God's kingdom is on display as we produce the fruit of the Christ-follower's character. God's Spirit desires and destines us for growth. As long as we live, we are to be fruitful. So what becomes of us when it comes our turn to die?

THE GARDEN STATE

In the Bible's great finale—the Revelation—we are given an extended glimpse of eternity. And what do we see? In Revelation, heaven is a city. But this new city has the feel of a garden. While urban, heaven echoes with Eden.

> Then he showed me the river of the water of life, clear as crystal, flowing from the throne of God and of the Lamb down the middle of the city's main street. The tree of life was on each side of the river, bearing twelve kinds of fruit, producing its fruit every month. The leaves of the tree are for healing the nations, and there will no longer be any curse.
>
> —Revelation 22:1–3

The tree of life has been restored! It bears twelve kinds of fruit. In the Bible, the number twelve signifies the people of God. Twelve sons of Jacob. Twelve tribes of Israel. Twelve disciples of Jesus. The twelve types of fruit tell us God will finally and fully satisfy his love-hungry people.

When we were cut off from Eden's fruit, we were left to crave something we could no longer have. But in the city of heaven, our famished souls will be satisfied with a buffet of God's loving provision. This is not the way it used to be. This is even better than it was before! God will feed us, and we will be filled. And there will be plenty for everyone.

Joyce Kilmer was a poet-soldier who died too young on a battlefield in World War I. Pictures from that era's war zones reveal man-made wastelands of destruction—bare landscapes and burned-out forests. But Kilmer imagined a greener world beyond the blasted and browned world he saw.

I think that I shall never see
A poem lovely as a tree.

A tree whose hungry mouth is prest
Against the earth's sweet flowing breast;

A tree that looks at God all day,
And lifts her leafy arms to pray;

A tree that may in Summer wear
A nest of robins in her hair;

Upon whose bosom snow has lain;
Who intimately lives with rain.

Poems are made by fools like me,
But only God can make a tree.[4]

Kilmer was on to something.

God planted a tree in a garden. Sin splintered it.

But not one to give up, God placed a new tree in another garden, and there he placed himself upon it. On Golgotha stands a cross—eternity's most fruitful tree. God's power on full display.

Now a final garden awaits our arrival. God resides there. His relationship and residence and rule will finally be restored and complete.

If I were a poet (and I am not) I would retouch Kilmer's lines to reflect the reality of sin and the promise of a new beginning.

Sin makes fools of people like me,
But thanks be to God, he has planted a tree.

TALK TO GOD

Lord God,
You created me to live for you and with you and within you.
Forgive my chasing of empty mirages
Instead of resting in your peace-giving Presence.

Make me your garden! Walk with me in the morning.
Stay near in the heat of the day.
Hold my hand when evening comes.
Amen.

TALK TO ONE ANOTHER

1. Read the account of Eden in Genesis 2:8-15. What stands out to you about this description of the garden?

2. Consider the Tolkien quote at the beginning of this chapter. He contends that our lives are "soaked with the sense of exile." In other words, no matter how much we improve ourselves and the world around us, we never feel fully at home. Do you agree or disagree with Tolkien? Why?

3. How is salvation through Jesus—a restored relationship with God—even better than returning to Eden?

LISTEN TO SCRIPTURE

Matthew 21:33–43
Luke 13:6–8
Revelation 2:7

SIX

A river went out from Eden to water the garden.

GENESIS 2:10

Eventually, all things merge into one,
and a river runs through it.

NORMAN MACLEAN, TWENTIETH-CENTURY
AMERICAN AUTHOR AND SCHOLAR

Twice I nearly drowned.

The first time I remember only vaguely given that I was no more than four or five years old. But a few snapshots still survive in my mind. My family was vacationing on the Gulf of Mexico. I was floating facedown in the water enveloped by blue. From the corner of my eye, my father's legs appeared. With one swift movement he pulled me topside. I am sure the event affected me because I refused to learn how to swim until I was well into my teenage years.

The second time was in college. I was working in Virginia for the summer. The pay was low and the hours were long. One day, I decided to cool off in the Rappahannock River on my way home from work. I was no more than fifty feet from shore when the current changed, becoming surprisingly strong. It took every bit of my strength to swim back to shore. If I had been a little farther out, the story might have ended differently. Even today when I hear of people caught in a swift current, I think back to those panic-filled moments and thank God that I was spared such a fate.

Truth be told, I have never felt at ease around water. Only God's sense of humor would choose a person who dreads water and destine them to be a Baptist pastor—one who must regularly stand in water as people confess their faith.

Water is powerful. And water is a powerful image in the pages of the Bible.

RIVERS RUN THROUGH IT

"A river went out from Eden" (Genesis 2:10). God's creative activity is still fresh in mind. Light has dawned. Dust has settled. Breath is bestowed. Garden is in full bloom. And four rivers, we are told, run through it. Don't think creeks. Don't imagine ambling streams or rambling rivers. Think lots of water, like the ocean. Think velocity, like the Rappahannock at flood stage. After all, Eden's one river fed four others, each spectacular in their own right.

Rivers essentially serve two purposes.

First, rivers provide. Find any city on a map and likely you will find it situated on a river. Why? Because the founders of the city knew that life depends on water. Our bodies need to drink. Our crops must be irrigated.

In the Bible, rivers carry life-giving water and more. Rivers carry the blessings of God to the people he loves. Genesis 1 drives home this point. The headwaters of Eden's rivers flowed into faraway lands filled with exotic riches. Gold and onyx and bdellium were in abundance. Scholars who understand the biblical languages better than I do, scratch their heads at this last element. One educated guess suggests bdellium is an ancient word for pearls.[1]

I grew up in western Texas, not known for its abundance of water. My hometown of San Angelo is nestled alongside the Concho River. The river is named after the conchs or freshwater mussels that make the river their home. These freshwater creatures produce an exquisite black pearl like none other in the world. Concho pearls are prized and pricey. In my mind, when I read bdellum, I think of black pearls—unique and valuable.

A river flowed through Eden. God's blessings flowed. God provided for his people. Blessings were in abundance.

A river's second purpose is to divide. Rivers bless, but they also create boundaries. My home state of Texas again serves as a simple example. Most of the state is given its shape by the Red River in the north and the Rio Grande in the south. One river divides two states. The other river divides two countries.

Rivers divide because of the simple fact that they are difficult to cross. The famous city of Oxford, England, takes its name from the place on the River Thames that was easiest for oxen to ford—that is, to cross. Do you see it? *Ox. Ford.* Rivers naturally divide, and this fact did not escape the attention of the first readers of Genesis.

In this sense, the Bible is written *for* us, but it is not written *to* us. We benefit from the Bible's truth and perspective and wisdom and insight into our God-made world. But we are not the writers' original audience. We can't say with any certainty that Moses had us in mind when he put Genesis onto parchment. His audience, as far as he knew, was a rag-tag group of refugees clawing their way up from slavery in Egypt, across a seemingly endless desert to a new home they only knew from promises made by God. In the desert, rivers are rare. Hearing of Eden's quartet of powerful rivers no doubt whet the appetite of the people's parched minds.

A water-crossing had inaugurated their trek. The Red Sea had parted in front of them as they put the land of Egypt in the rear-view mirror. And at their journey's end, a river was waiting for them. The people would cross the Jordan River, which divided the dry desert from their new country. A new life would commence once they crossed this boundary. No longer slaves, they would ford a river and find a home.

The old saying "up the river" is an expression meaning "to go to prison." The term is believed to have originated from Sing Sing prison, which is quite literally situated up the Hudson River from New York City. *Up the river* means to become a prisoner. For the ancient Hebrews, *across the river* translated into total freedom.

Like Eden, rivers run through the landscape of the Older Testament. Almost without exception these rivers remind us of the blessings of God, the barriers of life, or both.

Gideon stopped at a river before battle. How his men drank from the water signaled who was to be discharged and who was to charge with him into battle. God blessed Gideon with the right people to accomplish the task at hand (Judges 7).

Naaman was a military leader who suffered from leprosy. Leprosy was a disgrace, and as every soldier knows, honor is everything. Naaman made the trek from his home in Aram to meet the prophet Elisha in hopes of a cure. Elisha informed him that a miracle waited for him in the waters of the Jordan. All he had to do was wash. Naaman balked. The Jordan was a muddy creek compared to the majestic river of his native land. But wise counsel convinced Naaman to trust the simple instructions from God. Naaman found the blessing and cure he was looking for in a river (2 Kings 5).

David, the renaissance ruler—the poet-king of the Older Testament—returned to rivers again and again to explain his experience with God's goodness:

- "He leads me beside quiet waters," (Psalm 23:2).
- "As a deer longs for flowing streams, so I long for you, God," (Psalm 42:1).
- "I thirst for you," (Psalm 63:1).

In Montgomery, Alabama, a fountain stands as a monument to the civil rights workers of the 1960s. The words above the cascading fountain read, "Until justice rolls down like waters and righteousness like a mighty stream." The fountain attributes this quote to Martin Luther King, Jr. But King would tell us he drew these words from Amos 5:24. In Amos's days as in ours, we thirst for a world where all the wrongs of injustice are finally and forever put right.

PRINCE OF TIDES

So it should come as no surprise that the ministry of the Messiah began in a river. We know precious little of Jesus's early days. We are told only enough to make us curious. Silence defines the majority of Jesus's early life—years and years of silence. And then Jesus—quite literally—splashes onto the scene.

> Then Jesus came from Galilee to John at the Jordan, to be baptized by him. But John tried to stop him, saying, "I need to be baptized by you, and yet you come to me?"
>
> Jesus answered him, "Allow it for now, because this is the way for us to fulfill all righteousness." Then John allowed him to be baptized.
>
> —Matthew 3:13–15

As Jesus wades into the water, we witness both the giving of blessings and the crossing of barriers. Jesus—God in the flesh—steps into the river, which in turn carries him into our lives. Gold is rich. But God is richer. Pearls are pretty. But the presence of God is wealth on another order of magnitude. God's ultimate blessing is the gift of himself.

Jesus also crosses a barrier. The silence of thirty years is broken. From this moment on, Jesus's life is a public one. Jesus, like Moses of old, offers to lead his people out of sin's captivity, through the high desert of life's struggles, and into a new homeland of a restored relationship with God.

Every time I check my bag on an airline, I secretly wonder if I will ever see it again. (I know I can't be the only one to think this way.) In fact, every year 2 million of the over 400 million bags checked on U.S. airlines are misplaced. Somewhere between 50,000 to 100,000 are never reunited with their owners. What becomes of them? They go to Alabama.

Scottsboro, Alabama, is home to the Unclaimed Baggage Center. Items unfit for sale are tossed. Everything else is sold at a steep discount.[2] For years I have tried to convince my wife to add Scottsboro to our summer vacation itinerary, but to no avail. Can you imagine what someone's luggage might tell about a person?

At times we all feel like unclaimed baggage. It seems that no one is looking for us. Other people make us feel unfit or unwanted. We might even label ourselves a lost cause. So what joy it is to realize that God himself has been in search of us. He claims us for himself. Those who feel secondhand are of first concern to Jesus.

Jesus's public life began in a river. So, too, our public embrace of Jesus begins in water. Christian baptism takes many forms, but the message is the same: a barrier separating our old self from our new self has been crossed. Life is now lived under the blessing of God.

One of my most treasured memories is the baptism of my friend Jack. Jack was in his seventies and quite ill. During one of his countless hospital stays, Jack confided in me that while he had been a Christian for decades, he had never been baptized. With the end of life drawing near, what he had so long neglected was now of immediate importance. Jack requested I bring a container of water with me on my next hospital visit. It is important here to point out my Baptist tradition practices baptism only by total immersion, so to pour water to symbolize baptism was to be a new experience for me. But given the circumstance, I believed we were all doing the best we could. At the last moment, however, Jack demurred. Looking me square in the eye, Jack said, "I will be in church on Sunday. You can baptize me then. If I am going to do this, I want to do it right."

I admired his resolve, but I secretly doubted Jack would be out of the hospital, much less able to make it to church. I was surprised—better to say, astounded—when Jack showed up on time and ready to go. With the help of his two adult children we eased Jack into the pool, wheelchair and all, and slipped him gently beneath the water's surface. Jack died later that same week. But his funeral took on the same tone as his baptism: Jack's barriers were now all behind him. He was at last experiencing the uninterrupted blessings of being at home with his Savior.

Was this too much? Did Jack really need to go to all the trouble of baptism? The answer, as with many of life's mysteries, is both yes and no.

At the risk of sounding heretical, I find it hard to imagine God needs the literal act of our baptism. Our relationship with him is settled from the first moment we surrender our lives to him. Baptism is important not because God needs it, but because *we* need it. To enter the river of baptism and emerge on the other side is the defining moment we need to put aside our past self and to embrace the person we are destined to be in Christ.

In keeping with this symbol, the earliest Christians practiced baptism only once a year—on Easter. Men and women were baptized separately, and for a good reason: they were baptized naked. At the water's edge, the new Christian would drop their old clothes. Emerging from the far side of the water, the Christian community presented the convert with a new set of clothes. The old is gone and the new has come! (2 Corinthians 5:17). The new clothes served as a symbolic reminder that they were now clothed in Christ (Galatians 3:26–28).

I often remind those who are stubborn about the act of baptism that the only person who did not need baptism was Jesus himself. But we see him there, at Jordan's edge, telling John that what God deems necessary is never wrong.

WATER, WATER EVERYWHERE

For the longest time, I have admired a habit practiced by my Catholic brothers and sisters. Their worship begins at the doorway of the church when they dip their fingers into a fount of water and daub the sign of the cross across their body. In this moment they recall and relive their baptism. I am not suggesting all Christians should adopt this practice. But we would do well to understand the way water symbolizes our life in Christ. Water is needed for drinking and bathing. In these ways, water symbolizes our deepest spiritual needs.

Drinking

We all live on the edge of thirst. A few hours without water and we find it difficult to think about anything else. A scene from my childhood still holds a vivid place in my mind. One outdoor water fountain served the needs of my entire little league baseball team. At the end of practice we hot and thirsty boys would do whatever was necessary to be first in line for a drink. The water was tepid and tasted of old pipe, but we drank until we could hold no more. Thirst trumped taste.

Jesus compares the relationship he offers with God to water.

Through this metaphor, Jesus reveals his true importance. Jesus is not a mere add-on to the experience of a good life; he is essential for life itself. Without Jesus, true life is impossible.

Jesus said, "Whoever drinks from the water that I will give him will never get thirsty again," (John 4:14). Jesus claims to offer a satisfaction in life that no one or nothing else can provide. This would be a ridiculous claim if it were not for the fact that it is also true.

Accomplishment, applause, and affluence are incapable of satisfying our deepest desires. Many successful, famous, and wildly wealthy people are unhappy. Why? Could it be that those who "have it all" realize that the "all" they have obtained fails to satisfy the deepest thirst of the human soul?

An old seafarer's story tells of the crew of a sailing ship that had depleted their stores of fresh water while crossing the Atlantic. Hailing an oncoming vessel, they signaled for water. The reply came back, "Dip down and drink." The thirsty sailors did not realize they had already sailed into the wide mouth of the Amazon River, the fresh water of which flows far out beyond the first sight of land. Unbeknownst to the suffering sailors, they were floating in the very water they desperately needed.[3]

A fitting parable for our times! Our dehydrated and deprived souls are willing to gulp down anything that promises relief. All the while the only One who can truly satisfy us surrounds us as he waits patiently for us to drink.

Donald Whitney, a professor and author, says there are three types of spiritual thirst. First, there is *the thirst of the empty soul.* At best, this soul is temporarily satisfied by the pleasure of sex, power, sports, or entertainment. But each gulp only produces a stronger thirst. Second is *the thirst of the dry soul.* Unlike the first thirst, the person with a dry soul understands that Jesus is the only water that satisfies, but unintentional neglect or deliberate disobedience causes their soul to become parched and brittle. Finally, there is *the thirst of the satisfied soul*. This is the best of all thirsts—a soul having found contentment in Christ but at the same time craving more.[4]

Bathing

Water, when used on the inside, quenches our thirst. Water, when used on the outside, cleanses our dirtiness.

My wife loves me deeply, but there are times when I come into the house from hours in the yard covered with the detritus and odors of my work. I often couple a five-mile run with my chores, which exacerbates my less-than-appealing aura. My wife's nose immediately turns up as she points to the shower. If she says anything, it is typically a single-syllabled "Go." I deserve better than this, don't I? After all, I work in the yard to provide her with a beautiful home. I exercise to stay physically attractive for her and physically fit for a long life together. Why such contempt for my labors of love? Even though she knows the long-term benefits, in the short term, I reek. There is no plainer way to say it. And the short-term solution makes the long-term rewards so much sweeter.

As followers of a crucified Lord, we have been washed from the dirt of our disobedience and sin. The Bible speaks of Jesus's selfless sacrifice as a cleansing to be found nowhere else (Ephesians 5:26). But since we are not yet perfect, we are in constant need of purification.

Confession and repentance provide us the washing we need. While often used as synonyms, confession and repentance are two separate but equally essential acts. Confession is admitting, "I did it, and I was wrong." But repentance goes deeper. Repentance is saying, "I did it, and now I am ready to change." Both the humility of confession and the tenacity of repentance are beyond our ability to perform for ourselves. Only by the Holy Spirit and God's grace are we scrubbed from the filth of our unfaithfulness. "If we confess our sins, he is faithful and righteous to forgive us our sins and to cleanse us from all unrighteousness," (1 John 1:9). Cleansing is God's doing and ours for the asking.

Jonathan is a giant turtle that lives on the British territorial island of St. Helena in the South Atlantic Ocean. Jonathan is 190 years old. In 2016, British royalty came for a visit. Jonathan's caretakers, wanting him to look his best, used a loofah and surgical soap to scrub away nearly two centuries' worth of dirt from his shell. "He seemed to enjoy the whole experience," noted his caretaker.[5]

Like Jonathan, time has taken its toll on us. Our lives are barnacled with guilt, caked with regrets, and stained from our lack of integrity. Couple this with the reality that we are destined to meet royalty—Jesus. One day soon, we will be face to face with our king. The cleansing we require is more than what we can accomplish ourselves. The longer we live, the deeper the stains seem to penetrate. My best efforts make only superficial difference. I need a deeper scrub than what I can provide for myself. In Christ, my stench is removed, my stains resolved, and my life restored.

As Jesus hung dead on the cross, a soldier assigned to the detachment overseeing the day's executions, performed a grizzly duty. He plunged his sword into Jesus's side to confirm Jesus was indeed dead. Do you remember what happened? Blood poured out, as you might expect. But something else more surprising happened. "But one of the soldiers pierced his side with a spear, and at once blood and water came out. He who saw this has testified so that you also may believe. His testimony is true, and he knows he is telling the truth," (John 19:34–35).

The issue of water provides a medical clue to the cause of Jesus's death. But I believe the Gospel writer is concerned with more than a postmortem autopsy. Jesus's blood forgives. We sing and speak of this often. But what do we make of the water? Could this flow from the side of Jesus be a new river, fit for meeting our needs of drink and bath? The springs of Eden are reopened! The barrier of death is crossed. The blessing of God is ours. Water is everywhere and ours for the taking.

HIGH TIDE

The book of Revelation confuses many people with its jumble of images and visions. Others find Revelation too frightening to read with its future filled with anarchists and antichrists. But the reason Jesus revealed himself and parts of his plan to John was to encourage and embolden his followers (Revelation 22:7). How is it that our response to the Revelation is so opposite what the Lord originally intended?

Whenever I read Revelation, I remind myself to keep my focus more on Jesus and less on my interpretations of the end times. Seen this way, Revelation assures us that all will end well. Indeed, the final book of the Bible leaves us with an image of heaven reminiscent of Eden. And like Eden, a river runs through it.

> Then he showed me the river of the water of life, clear as crystal, flowing from the throne of God and of the Lamb down the middle of the city's great street.
>
> —Revelation 22:1–2

Typically, a river running down the middle of a street is a sign of disaster. If you have ever been in a flash flood, you know what I mean.

But rest assured such is not the case with heaven. Remember that Revelation speaks in symbols. This unusual description of heaven's river tells us that the blessing of God will flow straight from the King of Heaven directly to where his people live. We will no longer have to search for God's blessings; God's blessing will find us. We will never be thirsty or dirty again. God's people will be quenched and cleansed.

Nearly a millennia ago, during the Sung dynasty, Chinese artists painted a river only after they had committed every contour and bend to memory. Their hand-painted depictions expressed more than topography. Each piece of art reveals an intimate understanding of a river. The river had to first be known by heart before it was put to canvas. In more modern times, Mark Twain tells of the wheel boat pilot's ability to know the Mississippi by experience and feel. Sandbars and shoals invisible to the untrained eye were intuited by the pilot's experience.[6] Both the painter and the boatman tell of an intimacy with a river that goes beyond the natural senses.

So shall it be as we splash on the banks of that eternal river. There we will stand on the far bank with Christ. The river of God will be ours to experience and navigate for all of eternity. Thirst will only survive as a memory. The dirt of our past will be finally and fully washed downstream. We will know the intimacy of God's blessings as they flow forever over our satisfied souls.

TALK TO GOD

Lord God,
Your blessings tend not to trickle. They are a raging river!
Yet my soul suffers from a parched past.
Still your waters just enough that I may drink, bathe, and be new.

This world does all within its power to drain and dirty me.
While you offer to quench and cleanse.
I give you thanks.
Amen.

TALK TO ONE ANOTHER

1. Have you ever dreamed of living by water? If so, what is it about the water that you find so appealing?

2. What do you think it means to be spiritually thirsty? How would you describe the thirst of your own soul?

3. In John 7:37–39, Jesus says having faith in him means we will experience living water from within us. What does this mean for you?

LISTEN TO SCRIPTURE

Psalm 1
Isaiah 44:1–5
Revelation 7:16–17

SEVEN

And the Lord God commanded the man,
"You are free to eat from any tree of the garden,
but you must not eat from the tree of the knowledge
of good and evil, for on the day you
eat from it, you will certainly die."

GENESIS 2:16–17

When a man's stomach is full it makes
no difference whether he is rich or poor.

EURIPIDES, FIFTH-CENTURY BC GREEK POET AND PLAYWRIGHT

Consider how much of life happens around food.

Food is found at the birth of a child. I recall the afternoon my wife and I brought our last baby home from the hospital. Friends were waiting for us in our driveway with lasagna and salad in hand. The next night another family delivered food—lasagna and salad. The third night brought different friends but the same meal yet again. What the food lacked in variety it compensated for in affection (and carbohydrates). We consumed every mouthful with gratitude.

Food plays a part at weddings. When I was married a quarter-century ago, the guests' expectations were simple—cake and tri-colored mints. Today, however, convention demands the bride's family provide a full sit-down meal for the attenders. Stomachs are filled and pocketbooks are emptied because we all know the occasion is somehow incomplete without food.

Food makes a cameo again at funerals. In fact, when our church hosts a funeral, the first thing our organizers demand to know is how many family members will be expected for the meal after the memorial service.

Life's important events are made sweeter or at least less bitter when paired with calories. It's hard to imagine birthdays, anniversaries, parties, class reunions, and graduations without food. How many little league baseball teams have gone out for ice cream after a hard-earned victory or an unexpected loss? Food serves as both toast and tonic for life's most emotional events.

Do you need a conversation starter? Bring up the topic of food. Ask a person their favorite restaurant or favorite recipe. It won't be long before your taste buds find something in common with theirs.

Personally, I am a man of simple tastes. I love to talk hamburgers. It started when I was in grade school. I took a sack lunch to school on most days, but "hamburger day" was the grand exception. Now as an adult, when I visit a new city, I ask the locals for the must-try burger joint, the greasier the better. In Tulsa, I can share my top choices, but the truth is the best hamburgers in town are found in my wife's kitchen.

Just as food is ever-present in our world, food seems to appear on nearly every page of the Bible. Jacob manipulates his brother, Esau, over a steaming bowl of stew. The dietary laws of Exodus and Leviticus, mind-numbing as they seem to modern readers, are nothing less than a stroke of genius on the part of God. Kosher food must be chosen deliberately and prepared carefully. Every meal properly prepared would serve as a reminder that holiness is accomplished intentionally.

The land promised to the Israelite people was described as a land flowing with food—milk and honey—a land both substantial and sweet. God commanded Elijah to get up and eat because the journey ahead would be too much for him to handle otherwise. Daniel insisted on keeping kosher when he was far from home and the go-along-to-get-along pressure was at its strongest.

Peter dreamed of food descending from heaven. Peter's Jewish-trained mind expanded as God helped him see beyond the categories of clean and unclean foods. His worldview exploded when he realized the same is true of people. God loves all people, Jew and Gentile alike. Jesus himself delighted the common folk and scandalized the upper-crust religious of his day when he chose to eat with the very folks that proper people were told to avoid.

Yes, the Bible is filled with food.

NO SMALL POTATOES

Humans have a complex relationship with food. If we eat too much or too little of it, we die. The reports on obesity and diabetes and heart health remind us of the dangers of overindulgence. The news of people starving in other parts of the world should cause us to pause and pray about our personal priorities. Some people eat to live, and others live to eat, and then there are those who barely get to eat at all.

How fitting that the first temptation humanity faces centers on what—or, better, what *not*—to eat. As Adam becomes aware of his hunger, God issues his commands (and I elaborate for the sake of imagination): *Eat. Feast from the garden. But trust me when I tell you that at the center of this garden stands a tree that will do you no good. If you eat from it, death will be your dessert.*

God's first instruction gives us the opportunity to explore the workings of God's commands. In many ways, God's first command is a template for all his commands to follow. Consider two simple truths.

First, God's commands are clear. Certainly some of God's instructions prove a challenge to understand, but these tend to be the exception. Do you doubt this? Consider the Ten Commandments. God makes honesty and fidelity and respect for life plainly clear. If we choose to ignore these commands, we can't claim confusion as the excuse for our poor choices.

Jesus follows suit with his instructions. Indeed his Great Command is simple and direct. Love God. Love people. No confusion. Simple clarity. Jesus's best recorded message (Matthew 5, 6, and 7) is likewise clear about living a nonjudgmental, free-from-worry, refusing-to-seek-revenge kind of life.

Someone wise once told me, "You don't have to be the smartest person in the room; you just have to listen to the smartest person in the room." Great counsel! How much would our lives benefit from acknowledging God as the smartest person in our lives? When we listen to him, we live. When we disobey, we court only defeat and death. God's commands are not easy, but they are simple.

Second, God's commands give humanity the responsibility of personal choice. Our response to God is our responsibility! God wants us to think for ourselves. The trouble starts when we start thinking only *of* ourselves.

The worst advice we are given in regard to our choice-making goes something like this: *Listen to your heart.* While it looks innocent enough, this advice is more dangerous than it appears. As much as we want to trust our own intuition, an honest look at our decision-making ability reveals that it is wrong more often than not.

Recently, I was visiting a friend in the hospital. The hospital's cobbled-together buildings, sprawling campus, and multiple construction zones conspired against me as I tried to locate my friend's room. Increasingly frustrated, I ignored the directional signs and let my instincts guide me. It did not end well. I found myself at the far end of the hospital from where I needed to be. Much the same thing happens when we follow our desires through the labyrinth of decision-making. What feels right is often wrong. And what feels hard is often the exact thing we need to do.

Might I suggest a slight adjustment to this questionable counsel of following our hearts? Instead of listening *to* our hearts, would we do better to listen *with* our hearts? God invites us to tune our hearts to his instruction instead of our instinct and intuition.

Airline pilots are trained to do three things when flying in an emergency: aviate, navigate, and communicate—in that order. No matter what else is happening, the pilot must fly the plane, the pilot must choose a direction, and the pilot must let other people know what is happening. We need the same in times of crisis. We keep moving. We ask God for guidance, and we consult those people who help us discern God's voice from the voice in our own head.

EAT AND RUN

In Genesis 3, the devil introduces chaos into the simple clarity of God's commands. This is Satan's way of operating. God is clear. Satan causes confusion.

More than two decades ago, chess master Garry Kasparov squared off against a computer—IBM's Deep Blue—in a round of chess. Kasparov held twelve consecutive chess titles and was at the top of his game. Up to that time, no computer had defeated a person playing at Kasparov's level. If your experience is like mine, I am defeated regularly by the chess app on my handheld device. Trust me when I say this chess match was a newsmaker at the time.

Kasparov had defeated Deep Blue only a year earlier. There was no reason to believe the outcome of this match would be any different. Yet, the deciding game that brought Deep Blue's victory over Kasparov lasted a mere hour. Deep Blue sacrificed its bishop and rook to capture Kasparov's queen. Kasparov realized he had lost control of the board. He conceded defeat for the first time in his career, later confessing, "I lost my fighting spirit."[1]

The conversation recorded in Genesis 3 feels like the back-and-forth of a chess match. We have a front-row seat to this duel of shattered nerves, misplaced moves, and misplayed opportunities. The record of Satan's first temptation gives us precious insight into the way Satan still tempts us today in attempts to seize control of the board.

Satan opens by misquoting God. He twists God's word just enough to call God's character into question. *Did God really say what I was told he said? Did he tell you that you couldn't eat from* any tree *in this beautiful garden? How dare he! Who does he think he is!*

The fact is God did not forbid eating from the trees of the garden. He only forbade the eating from one particular tree. Satan had the wrong information, or so Eve might have thought. In response, Eve immediately goes on the defensive. Eve may have felt it was her duty to defend God's reputation. Her intent was noble, but she was entering into a conversation she would be better off not having at all.

Even after Eve thinks she has cleared the matter up, Satan presses on. *If God has permitted you to eat from any tree in the garden, then why is this one tree in the center off limits? I don't understand, do you?*

Satan's second move is to manipulate God's clear commands, making them sound like a contradiction to common sense. *Death from a tree that looks like all the others? Help me understand!*

Satan offers the I-don't-get-it argument. To be honest, many of God's commands seem to make no sense to our rational minds in the heat of temptation. We want to follow our hearts! We want what we want, and too easily we convince ourselves that the consequences God warns us about don't apply to us.

Satan's third move is making God look like the guilty party. *God must be up to something! Eve, I don't think he is telling you the whole story. God doesn't want you to have the fruit not because it is bad for* you *but because it is bad for* him. *If you eat the fruit, you will be more like God, and that scares him.*

Satan still uses these same tired strategies today. He does so because they work. We fall for them time and again. Satan's strategy, much like that of Deep Blue's, is to seize control. His misquotes and his doubt-raising and his finger-pointing are designed to defeat our fighting spirit and to deflate our confidence in the goodness of God. The conversation between Eve and Satan, seen as a whole, renders two insights.

1. *Satan twists God's positive commands by focusing our minds on the negative.*

   God offers an entire garden for human enjoyment, but Satan emphasizes what is off-limits. The feast is forgotten as Eve obsesses over the forbidden.

   Doesn't Satan still use envy in the same way to torture our minds? God asks we simply trust him to provide all we need and all we can handle. But instead of focusing on what God sees fit to share with us, we focus on the things we don't have or the opportunities we haven't experienced. The mind being manipulated by Satan sees only what others have that we don't. The mind in touch with God sees the abundance of all we are given that we never deserved in the first place.

2. *Satan twists God's negative commands by focusing on the positive.*

   Consequences are downplayed. The cost is not considered much less counted. The destructive results are, at least for the moment, conveniently ignored.

   Infidelity lures us with this line of reasoning. How many marriages exchange a lifetime of rich relationship for the cheap thrill of a one-night stand? The promise of momentary gratification ignores the long-term pain we will

> cause ourselves and others. Our own minds seem to conspire against us. We ignore the real-life consequences to our ill-considered decisions by hoping that the obvious consequence of our own decisions somehow won't find us out.

Eve is playing soul-chess with a temptation machine. Try as she may, she will never win.

Are we, therefore, helpless in the face of temptation? Hardly. We have already discussed the fact that God's commands are typically simple. Indeed, the instruction on how to deal with Satan's temptations is a case in point. One of the most direct books in the New Testament, the book of James, offers this clear guidance: "Therefore, submit to God. Resist the devil, and he will flee from you," (James 4:7).

To address temptation, our first priority is to fall in love with God. We submit to God not because he demands our submission but because he deserves our submission. We yield to God's better judgment because we trust he has our best interest always in mind. This loyal love is our greatest protection. My marriage is at its best, not when I am intent on avoiding adultery, but when I focus on being in love with the one woman who is my wife.

Aspire to fall in love with God. Grow in admiration of God's character. Trust God's desire to save us from a world of self-inflicted pain. And when Satan calls God's character into question by second-guessing God's clear commands, we will see through Satan's half-truths and bald-faced lies.

A second priority should be that our only response to Satan need be a single word: *No!* With the same measure we submit to God, we resist the devil. To God we always say *yes*, and to Satan we need only say *no*.

Years ago, I took my staff to a self-defense training seminar. At the time, violence was on the rise in the city where I serve. Our church is located in an urban setting, so I thought it wise to be as prepared as possible to protect ourselves and the people under our care. The first session was a lesson on how to say no. A stern face and a firm voice sends an unmistakable message to a would-be attacker—*I refuse to be an easy target.* My favorite moment was watching our preschool and children's ministers—people trained to be nothing but pleasant—attempt to put on their mean faces. This is the best and most biblical approach to Satan.

Instead of a simple no, Eve over-reacts. In her panic, she puts words into God's mouth, "God said that we must not eat the fruit of that tree *or even touch it*" (Genesis 3:3, emphasis mine). Eve credits God for something God never said. Read God's original command again for yourself in Genesis 2. God never forbade Adam or Eve to touch the fruit. Granted, not touching the fruit is probably a good idea, but the fact remains that God never said it.

So, what was Eve doing? Instead of following God, Eve was creating her own rules. Eve's overreach reminds us that there are two ways to run from God. The first we know all too well. Let's call it—get ready for a big word—licentiousness. We give ourselves license to do as we please. We follow our heart, no matter what God or anyone else says to us. Licentiousness throws off restraint.

But running from God—and we see it here with Eve—also takes the form of legalism. Instead of bad behavior driving a wedge in our relationship with God, we allow our good behavior to create distance between us and our Creator. In the moment, Eve is no longer relating to God. She is relating to her rules about God. This worship of rules is a pious idol, but an idol nonetheless.

Ultimately licentiousness and legalism originate from our desire to supervise ourselves rather than our deep need to surrender to God. Rules can be controlled; God cannot. Rules feel safe; God is dangerous. Rules do our thinking for us; God requires we remain open to the Spirit's leading. Rules are one-size-fits-all; revelation means our relationship with God will grow with time and experience.

EAT YOUR FILL

I am mysteriously drawn to the odd scientific studies that delve into the minutia of life. For instance, have you ever wondered how, despite our best efforts, our shoelaces always manage to untie themselves? Luckily, there is a study that explains it!

Engineers at the University of California set out to solve this mysterious unraveling. They concluded that shoelaces untie themselves in a two-step process. First, the foot's impact with the ground loosens the knot ever so slightly. Second, the g-forces exerted on the laces as a walker swings his legs back and forth are comparable to the g's experienced on a high-speed roller coaster. The pounding and swinging collaborate to unravel even the best-tied shoestrings.[2]

God created us to be united with him. But the impact of sin and the stress of ongoing disobedience unravel the once-tight relationship. Now our relationship with God is frayed and ill-fitting.

The ongoing feast with God among the trees of the garden is no longer humanity's to enjoy. Ironic, isn't it? Adam and Eve's act of eating left them famished, and we inherited their hunger. In our crazed state of hunger, we willingly try anything to fill our emptiness.

The ancient author of Ecclesiastes shares his experience with us. Solomon in all his wisdom was baffled by how his education, affluence, and endless partying proved insufficient to satisfy the deepest hunger of his heart. Though the times have changed, people haven't. What ancient Solomon sampled three thousand years ago are the same things we in vain look to today in hopes of satisfaction. Wealth, accomplishment, and the promise of a good time define the desires of the modern life. But as it proved empty for Solomon, it will ultimately prove empty for us as well.

What, if anything, can satisfy the deep hunger of the human heart?

In the Gospels Jesus is very often pictured sitting at a dinner table. Years ago, I walked my church through the Gospels, stopping at every instant Jesus sat himself at a table to share a meal with other people. We stopped quite frequently!

Jesus sits at a table with Matthew, a tax-collector-turned-disciple, and his good-time buddies. Jesus reclines at the table of a high-profile Pharisee as a low-brow woman with a doubtful reputation is reduced to tears at Jesus's feet. Jesus ate with a jaded money collector named Zacchaeus who most considered a lost cause. This man was as short in height as he was on character, but Jesus spent an entire afternoon assuring him anyone can change by the grace of God.

But one meal among all the meals Jesus shared in his time on earth takes the cake.

On the day before Jesus's self-sacrifice, he pulled himself up to a table with his closest friends. They shared an ancient meal called Passover. The meal recreates the swirl of events of the Jews' emancipation from Egyptian slavery. Jesus summoned two elements of this ancient meal and pressed them into service by giving them fresh meaning. One was wine. The other was bread.

As he held the bread before his hungry followers, Jesus gave a command that echoes with Eden. "Eat," he said. And they ate their fill.

I am overwhelmed by the thought that one of God's first commands is identical to the same command Christ gives to his followers around the table. In Genesis, God offers the gift of eternal life. Through Christ, God offers the same gift yet again. In the garden, God offers fruit. At the table, Christ offers his flesh. The God of the garden and the Christ of the table (one in the same) offer their food for free. Though at no cost to us, this food of the Savior's flesh came at a high price to him.

Around this table with his disciples, Jesus says to all his would-be followers that he is the only one capable of satisfying the deep hunger of the human heart. Even today, as Jesus-followers share this meal, we remind ourselves that only Jesus fills the famished life. Whenever we approach the communion table, whether we call it the Eucharist or the Lord's Supper, our presence is itself a confession that our starving souls find satisfaction only in Christ. Because we belong to Christ, we will never go hungry again. Charles Spurgeon once observed, "Nothing teaches us about the preciousness of the Creator as much as when we learn the emptiness of everything else."[3] Indeed, it is at the table that we taste and see the Lord is good. Having tasted him, our lesser appetites lose their appeal.

While on safari in Africa, our tour guide informed us elephants seldom die naturally of old age. If not killed by people or predators, elephants will eventually die of starvation. It works this way: All elephants are born with six sets of molars. As each set wears out, it is replaced by the next in line. Eventually, all six sets of molars are discarded and only the elephant's gums remain. It's not long before the elephant's gums are blistered and tender. The elephant chooses to ease the pain in its mouth rather than address the emptiness of its stomach. It stops eating and waits for death to come. The elephant is too old to eat.

Such is not the case with us! We are never too old, and it is never too late to accept the invitation of Jesus to find the nourishment we so desperately need. God formed us. Only God can feed us.

In heaven we will continue the feast! Our minds often imagine heaven as a place of choirs and harps. But the Bible offers a very different picture. We will sit with our Savior and banquet in his presence. Best of all, we do not need to wait for the "one day" of heaven. The celebration begins at the moment we agree with God that only Jesus will sate our hungry hearts.

The invitation stands.

Pull up a chair.

Take off your load.

Scoot next to your Savior.

Eat.

TALK TO GOD

Lord God,
You nourish the famished—which I am!
The empty calories of popularity and prosperity and pride
Have made me hungrier for true sustenance.

Christ! Invite me to sit at your table.
With chaliced wine and plated bread
Satisfy my deepest need for you.
Amen.

TALK TO ONE ANOTHER

1. What are some of your most treasured memories that include food? Is it a food from your childhood or a food made by a special loved one? What about it makes these memories so powerful?

2. How do you view food? Has it become an idol you worship? Has it become an enemy you avoid? Is it a bit of both?

3. When Satan tempted Jesus in the desert, one of his specific temptations included food (Matthew 4:3–4). What do you think this temptation tells us about our nature and our natural weaknesses?

LISTEN TO SCRIPTURE

Psalm 34:8
Psalm 63:5
Matthew 9:9–13
Revelation 3:20

EIGHT

Then the LORD God said, "It is not good for the man to be alone. I will make a helper corresponding to him."

GENESIS 2:18

If I am a legend, then why am I so lonely?

JUDY GARLAND, TWENTIETH-CENTURY AMERICAN ACTRESS AND SINGER

At the seven-year mark of ministry together, my church gave me a much-needed sabbatical. My wife and I are both savers by nature, and over the years of our marriage we had managed to put enough money aside to take our entire family to Europe. Travel is the best education in my opinion. Our children still benefit today from what they experienced and learned during our time overseas. Michelangelo's *David*, Big Ben, and the waterways of Venice were among the art, architecture, and beauty we experienced.

At the end of our trek across the Old World, I had arranged for my family to return to the United States while I remained in England for two additional weeks of independent study. I am ashamed to admit that on several occasions over the course of our summer—especially on the days when a child threw a temper tantrum or my wife and I had tried one another's nerves—I secretly longed for my time of solitude and study.

The day finally arrived! I settled my family aboard their train destined for Heathrow Airport. After our final hugs and kisses, I stood on the platform and watched the train pull away. The train slipped down the track becoming no more than a speck of light in a dark tunnel. Then the light itself disappeared. To say that I was unprepared for what happened next is an understatement. Loneliness, in an uncontrollable wave, washed over me. I was surrounded by people, but I felt deeply and profoundly alone. To this day, I still consider this moment as the loneliest of my life.

What for me was a momentary experience, for many people is a daily reality. Loneliness is the emotional epidemic of our time. Half of Americans admit to being lonely. Thirteen percent of people say they have not a single person in their life who knows them well. *No one.* The results? Lonely people live shorter lives, experience more insomnia, and tend to adopt more unhealthy practices.[1] I wonder how many of the issues in our culture—from suicide to alcoholism to drug abuse to overeating to acts of violence—are the result of loneliness.

The Bible reveals life as it is. So, it is no surprise loneliness plagued many people in the pages of Scripture.

Jacob spent a night alone at the Peniel River. Jacob sent his travel party across the river. He was left by himself. The next day he would find himself face-to-face with his estranged brother, Esau. Perhaps Jacob needed space to think. There, alone in the dark, a stranger pounced upon him. Was this a thief? Was this Esau making a preemptive strike? No, it was the Lord. In Jacob's loneliness, God had been there all along.

Jeremiah was an unpopular prophet. His own people thought him unpatriotic. At his lowest point, Jeremiah was deposited into the bottom of a cistern. Made to hold water, this cistern now held a lonely man being punished by others for doing what God had instructed him to do.

Jesus himself experienced loneliness. Before commencing three years of public ministry, he spent forty days alone in the desert. In his solitude, Jesus was more vulnerable to temptation—as we all are. Let's just say that Satan took full advantage of Jesus's situation (Matthew 4:1-11).

ONE IS THE LONELIEST NUMBER

In Genesis 2 we meet Adam as he suffers from his own bout with loneliness. Even though Adam had never met another human being, he instinctively knew there was something not quite right about his solitary condition.

While writing this chapter, I visited a friend serving his sentence in a federal penitentiary. After making my way through the labyrinth of background checks and ID verification and drug residue tests, we finally sat face-to-face. We talked about what he misses most from the outside world. His favorite steak house and his childhood swimming hole topped the list. He also told me the first thing he will do when released is get a full body massage from a professional masseuse. My friend misses gentle human contact. When prisoners or guards touch him, it is typically in violence. My friend longs for compassionate touch. My friend is lonely.

Loneliness is a prison, and Adam was doing time in solitary, until God intervened.

Comedians have often quipped that "I am" is the shortest sentence in the English language while "I do" is the longest sentence. Marriage is a worthy theme to explore as we witness the meeting of Adam and Eve. However, the events of Genesis 2 transcend this noble topic. More is at play.

Throughout the act of creation, God regularly looked upon what he made and noticed its goodness. Genesis 1:4 gives an example: "God saw that the light was good . . ." Such appreciation occurs seven times. But when confronted with Adam's sense of aloneness, God agreed with Adam that his situation was "not good" (Genesis 2:18). God created Adam from the rich loam of Eden. God decided to craft Eve using a rib from Adam himself. Is God hinting that people, especially a man and his wife, live best when they walk side by side?

What does all this tell us? God is certainly all we *need.* But God himself recognizes that he is not all we *want.* Life can be endured when alone, but life is savored when shared. Living alone is like water. Living with others is like wine. The first is survival; the second is a celebration.

Some people describe the experience of discovering a "second self," a person who understands them in ways that transcend words or explanation. Could this be the Adam-instinct in all of us, longing for another person who knows us only in the way we know ourselves?

In 2001, a young girl named Laura Buxton hatched an odd plan. From her home in Staffordshire, England, she wrote her name on a luggage tag, tied it to a helium balloon, and released it into the English sky. The balloon traveled some 140 miles before finally descending upon Wiltshire, England. The remains of the balloon and the luggage tag were discovered by another young lady (get ready for this!) named Laura Buxton. Both Laura Buxtons are the same age. They have the same hair color. Both Lauras own Labrador retrievers, guinea pigs, and rabbits. Talk about an unlikely way of discovering a second self![2]

Don't we all send up such trial balloons? We seem always on the lookout for someone who "gets us." To find them relieves our sense of loneliness in the world. Some people find their second self in a sibling, a spouse, a dear friend, or even one of their children. When someone discovers their second self, Adam's words become our own:

> This one, at last, is bone of my bone
> and flesh of my flesh.
> —Genesis 2:23

At last! At last, someone I can trust! At last, a person who understands my deeper parts! At last, God has given me a person who shares his image and who shares my imagination. At last, I am no longer alone!

The Chinese language, like English, combines words that when joined mean something different than either of the original words. The Chinese symbol for *man* when joined with the Chinese symbol for *woman* results in the Chinese word meaning *good.* This is the message we receive from the garden when Adam and Eve find themselves together. God is with the man and woman. And the man and woman are with one another. Communion and community. This is paradise.

ALL THE LONELY PEOPLE. WHERE DO THEY ALL COME FROM?

Sin breaks relationships. This is the real tragedy of Adam and Eve's sin. Relationships once whole and holy are now broken and sullied. In their shame, the two humans hide from God. When God brings down the curse, he is only articulating the consequences already brought to bear on Adam and Eve's relationships (Genesis 3:16–19). One word sums up God's judgment: Loneliness.

Noted Dutch psychiatrist J. H. van den Berg said, "If loneliness didn't exist, we could reasonably assume that psychiatric illness would not either."[3] Yet both do exist, and in abundance. Everywhere we are surrounded by crowds of people, but within the throng we feel alone.

I pastor a church where 1,500 people come in and out the doors each week. Despite the number, the most common complaint I hear is, "I don't know anyone and nobody seems to care about me."

Gently, I confront people with an unpleasant truth: loneliness is a consequence of the world we live in. However, it may also be that loneliness is something we choose. Many people who bemoan their lonely condition often refuse to risk the vulnerability and boldness required to form new relationships. It is easier to sooth ourselves by pointing the finger at others rather than face the truth of our own reluctance and fears.

There are no easy answers to our loneliness. But there are some difficult questions that need to be asked. More than exploring these two questions, we must allow these two questions to explore us.

First, am I using people to avoid God?

We live in a fast-paced world. When asked how I am doing, my go-to response is, "Busy!"

Imagine, if you can, driving your car with no brake pedal. Picture the terror of controlling the speed of a vehicle with only the gas pedal at your disposal. Frightening, isn't it? Yet, this is the very way many of us live our lives. We accelerate from work to school to soccer practice to meetings. On top of this, we multitask. On average we check our smartphones once every 4.3 seconds of our waking lives.[4] And the church only adds to our chaos. I have fantasized, yet I have never been brave enough to do it, of canceling all church activities with the exception of worship for an entire month in order to encourage people to slow down. But the truth is, most folks would fill the void with some other activity. Like the imaginary car without a brake, the only time we stop is when we crash.

We shake our heads at Adam and Eve as they hid from God in the garden. But do we bury ourselves under our busy schedules for the same reason? Deep down is a truth we don't want to admit to ourselves: we are running from our own emptiness. Yet our heavily populated schedules will never satisfy our lonely souls.

Exodus 18 finds Moses in a leadership dilemma. The Israelite community had become too dependent on his leadership. They stood in line before him, like a justice-dispensing vending machine. No doubt they told each other as they stood in line: "No one can interpret God's law like Moses!" Moses's father-in-law saw what Moses did not. Moses could not maintain this pace of leadership and maintain peace with God.

But as a leader, I wonder, did Moses like it this way? As much as he might have chaffed against the people's constant demand for attention, did he secretly enjoy being needed? I experience days when no one calls in a crisis or no one sends me an email asking for my advice. I slump into a strange malaise. I want people to need my calm and counsel.

Like Moses, we should ask ourselves, *Has my intense schedule become a method of avoiding God? Am I using my work for God as an excuse to ignore him? Is my overdependence on people a sign that I no longer know how to depend on God? Am I afraid to hit the off switch?*

Four times a year, I make my way to a monastery not far from where I live. The fifty or so monks who live at Clear Creek live at a pace that makes room for God. They are guided by *The Rule of Saint Benedict*. Although *The Rule* has been around for 1,500 years, it is my opinion that it has never been more relevant than it is today.

During my three or four days at Clear Creek, I live by the unofficial mantra of the monastic life: *ora et labora*—pray and work. Yet every time I drive through the gates of Clear Creek, I experience a sense of dread. What do I do with myself now that no one needs me? But once the withdrawal symptoms of my overscheduled mind passes, I remember again God doesn't want anything *from* me. He wants *me*. With my slower pace, I find the peace no packed schedule can provide. I remember again God made me for himself before he made me for anything or anyone else. I need other people, to be sure, but I need to remember people and their demands are poor substitutes for God's rich presence.

Unfortunately, some people do not discover this until it is too late. Here again, my experience as pastor provides my examples. A couple divorces. For the woman, her husband was her world. Now her world has left orbit and revolves around the warm glow of another woman. She is alone.

After a lifetime of service, a man retires. He once saw himself as the smartest person in the room, but now with a gold watch in hand he is put out to pasture. No one calls. He is not consulted. His work is gone and with it some part of his identity.

In my previous book, I wrote of my father's weeks-long stay in the ICU of my hometown hospital. As he lingered dangerously close to death, our family decided that there would not be a moment when my father would be left alone. Even when he was unconscious, we spoke words of encouragement. We asked questions of the medical personnel. My brother and I took turns keeping nighttime vigil next to our father's bed in a chair designed solely for the purpose of depriving the sitter of sleep. I recall walking down the ICU corridor on more than one occasion and seeing room after room of patients who were entirely alone. In fact, I noticed some rooms and patients that never received a visitor. At such moments aloneness is a frightening reality.

How do we deal with such aloneness? Whether by the choice of another or by circumstances beyond control, we will all face abandonment at some point in life. If we have used people to avoid God, when the people in our life are suddenly stripped away from us, we then realize we have no one from which to draw strength.

Indeed, many people in the Bible dealt with desertion. The Older Testament Joseph was very nearly murdered by his brothers. He found himself sold into slavery, alone among the odd Egyptians with their strange language and peculiar customs. Paul, the man who wrote much of our New Testament, faced abandonment near the end of his life. In 2 Timothy 4:16–17 he says, "At my first defense, no one stood by me, but everyone deserted me. . . . But the Lord stood with me and strengthened me." Jesus himself was abandoned. Betrayed by Judas, detained by the powers that be, and deserted by his fair-weather followers, Jesus faced execution alone.

Although unwelcomed, abandonment affords the opportunity to practice two spiritual disciplines.

First, abandonment gives us the occasion to *practice forgiveness.* Henri Nouwen said, "Forgiveness is the name of love practiced among people who love poorly."[5] Desertion tests the depths of our ability to pardon others. Another person's poor practice of love does not excuse our failure to practice forgiveness. The mistakes inflicted by others upon us give us the opportunity to imitate the very same forgiveness lavished on us by God when we deserved it least.

Second, abandonment provides the opportunity to *greater dependence on God.* People who endure abandonment tell me that while they never want to experience such a thing again, they are grateful for the intimacy with God that resulted from their desertion.

At one point or another, most of us have used people to avoid God. But unless we are careful, we may overcorrect and drift to a second extreme, which requires the asking of a second uncomfortable question.

Am I using God to avoid people?

God is certainly all we need for salvation. But God is not all we need for our personal satisfaction. Do you disagree with this statement? If God alone could have met every need of the first man's heart, then Adam would never have craved Eve, and God might never have created her. At issue is not the sufficiency or insufficiency of God. We must simply acknowledge the way we are made. We are designed to desire God. We are also built to crave community with other people. Typically, extroverts tend to use people to avoid God. Introverts, on the other hand, are tempted to use God to avoid other people. As a world-class introvert, I know what I am talking about.

It often surprises people when I confess to being an introvert. True, I have chosen an extroverted profession, but my natural disposition is quieter than my public persona lets on. An extrovert receives energy from being with people; an introvert refuels by spending time alone.

I can honestly say my intimacy with God in solitude is far greater than what I typically experience when I am around other people. My private study at home provides me more connection with God than the worship center at my church. I choose weekly worship as a much-needed discipline, but I delight in times of solitude in the presence of God.

The biblical examples of aloneness with God are too many to recount. Jacob, mentioned earlier in this chapter, wrestled with God at Peniel (Genesis 32). It was there that a swindler was transformed into a humbler man. From this point on, Jacob would no longer strut through life. Instead, he walked with a limp. John, one of the original disciples, first followed Jesus when he was in his teenage years. Near the end of his life, John is alone, exiled on the rocky island of Patmos. John now wears the clothes of an old man. One Sunday while in private worship, John hears a voice he had not physically heard in close to seven decades. But he knew who it was. In that moment, John's exile is transformed into a place of intimacy (Revelation 1:12–13).

Jesus himself sought escape from the public eye. He found more energy in time alone with his Father than what a few extra hours of sleep could give him (Mark 1:35). Emilie Griffin, a contemplative Christian author says, "Solitude is one way we imitate Jesus."[6] I agree.

Yet, as an introvert, I need the regular reminder that if my deep involvement with God leads me to ignore the needs of people, I am violating the very heart of the Jesus I claim to follow. My love of God must include love for others or else my professed love for God is only a clever spiritual disguise. The God who invites me to savor his presence also commands me to serve others in the throes of life's struggles.

I can't help but think of Mary and Elizabeth, both of whom had been told to expect babies. The two pregnancies were miracles—Elizabeth's because of her and her husband's advanced age, and Mary because no husband was involved to begin with. A late-in-life pregnancy can be explained, but a pregnancy without intercourse requires a bit more faith to accept. Mary, at this most mysterious and mind-boggling moment of life, might well have been tempted to retreat into herself. We would all understand if she pulled back and stayed close to home. But Mary moved in the opposite direction of her instinct. Mary stepped out and stepped in to serve Elizabeth for the duration of her geriatric pregnancy. Mary's spirituality was deepened not by isolation but through engagement.

As a pastor I hear people say things such as, "I do not need a church. I can worship God when I am backpacking in the woods" or "I've been hurt by Christians, and I don't want to risk that again." These types of statements, as genuine as they may feel in the moment, neglect other, more enduring truths. Worship among other people expands our compassion in a way private worship cannot. And for those who have been wounded, I offer this: don't let the person who hurt you win! We must resist allowing our personal hurts to rob us of the satisfaction our hungry hearts crave in corporate worship. Indeed, to cut ourselves off from imperfect people requires that we stop going anywhere where people are involved—which is everywhere! We must see the temptation to use God to avoid people for what it is—a decision made with only self-preservation in mind.

IT'S LONELY AT THE TOP

So what are we to do if we find ourselves alone? Despite your best efforts and in spite of other people's good intentions, at some time in our lives most of us will experience the train leaving the station or we will find ourselves in solitary confinement or we will lay helpless and unattended in a hospital room.

From his own experience, I believe Jesus's voice echoes across the ages offering two comforting words to every lonely heart: "I understand."

On the eve of his crucifixion Jesus said, "Indeed, an hour is coming, and has come, when each of you will be scattered to his own home, and you will leave me alone. Yet I am not alone, because the Father is with me," (John 16:32). Jesus was abandoned by the very people who had promised to follow him come what may.

But Jesus still had God, right? Here the answer is a bit more complicated. Theologians have wrestled for centuries with Jesus's words from atop the cross: "My God, my God why have you abandoned me?" (Matthew 27:46). Was God absent at the moment of his son's death?

My answer is a definitive yes and no.

God the Father was *in fact* present at Jesus's death. It's hard to imagine him being anywhere else. What Christ's words tell us is that Jesus couldn't *feel* God at the moment of his death. Jesus's emotional response to the depth of human sin and the weight of God's justice hindered his ability to sense God's presence in the moment. Jesus felt—which is to say he *was*—very much alone.

Lonely from the top of his cross, Jesus places his aching heart near our own. If we listen closely enough, we can imagine him saying to us, *I understand. Me too. I know what you are going through because I have been there myself.*

Jesus's voice reminds us that in our lonely moments, God is closer than we think. When God feels farthest away, he is, in fact, closest at hand. We must learn to trust God's consistent character rather than our own unpredictable emotions.

ALONE IN A CROWD

Benjamin Kyle is a tragic figure. A missing person, he lives in Savannah, Georgia. How, you may wonder, can a person be missing if we know where he lives? In 2004, Kyle woke up behind the dumpster of a fast-food restaurant with no memory of his life up to that moment. Since then, only snatches of memory have returned. Adding insult to injury, no one has come forward to claim him. Benjamin Kyle is as alone as anyone can get.[7]

In Christ, we are invited to remember who we are and reclaim our true identity. God is looking for us. Indeed, he will not give up his search until we are home once again with him.

Of all the chapters in this book, this chapter is the most difficult to find an easy place to end. But I feel it would be disingenuous to put a nice, neat bow on loneliness. May it be enough for now to know that we will not be lonely forever. We will all one day meet the Lord who cures all loneliness, and we will hear Adam's words from our own lips as we exclaim in satisfied glory, "At last."

TALK TO GOD

Lord God,
You are in a category all by yourself—Alone.
And I feel much like most other people—alone.
From my solitary consignment, deliver me.

You do not desire that my life
Remain distant from yours.
I am my true self when we are close together.
Amen.

TALK TO ONE ANOTHER

1. Jesus often withdrew to be alone with his Father. How might you practice this discipline of solitude with God in your own life?

2. How do you respond to being alone? What do you enjoy about solitude and what makes you uncomfortable?

3. Even Jesus didn't handle life alone. He was born into a family. He surrounded himself with friends. What is it about our human nature that many people try to handle life alone?

4. Who are some lonely people you see in your daily life? What are some intentional ways you can engage in a relationship with them?

LISTEN TO SCRIPTURE

Psalm 68:5–6
Ecclesiastes 4:9–12
Mark 15:33–37

NINE

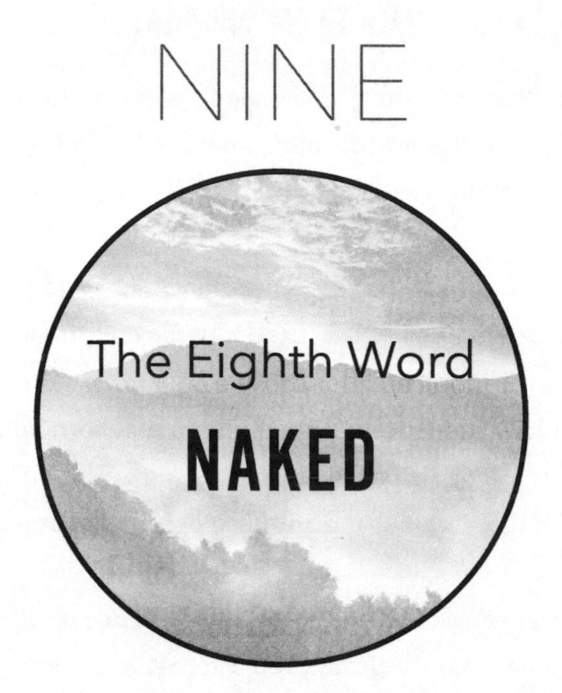

Then he asked, "Who told you
that you were naked?"
GENESIS 3:11

"I'm never wearing them,"
Ron was saying stubbornly. "Never."
"Fine," snapped Mrs. Weasley. "Go naked.
And Harry, make sure you get a picture of him.
Goodness knows I could do with a laugh."
J. K. ROWLING, AUTHOR OF THE HARRY POTTER SERIES

When will I stop having that nightmare?

If I had to guess, you probably have your own rendition of this same dream. In my version, I am standing on the platform of my church on a Sunday morning ready to teach. Suddenly, I discover I am not dressed. Your dream may differ in some of the details, but one theme remains constant—nakedness. This old familiar dream reveals something of our fear of vulnerability and embarrassment.

When "naked" first appears in the Bible, it is not a dream or a nightmare. It's a simple reality. "Both the man and his wife were naked, yet felt no shame," (Genesis 2:25). It seems odd that the Bible would go out of its way to tell us Adam and Eve did not need (or want) clothes. Why this detail?

The point is this: Adam and Eve had no secrets. They knew everything there was to know about one another. Their relationships knew no superficiality. They were at perfect ease with each other and with the Lord. Nothing inauthentic. Only transparency.

CUT FROM THE SAME CLOTH

My wife and I have known each other for three decades. My job as a husband is to be the world's greatest living expert on the one woman I call my wife. I know Paula's idiosyncrasies, her habits, and her moods, and she knows mine. I know her ways almost as well as my own, and I love her all the more. But as a complex person created as a unique expression of the image of God, I need more than one lifetime to know her fully.

A few months ago, I had a dream. (Yes, another dream. But at least this time, I was fully clothed!) I was back in high school, and I was participating in a state competition. The next morning, I shared my dream with my wife.

"I dreamed I was back in Corpus Christi in 1988 competing with my school."

"Wait. What?" Paula said. "*I* was in Corpus in 1988."

"I competed in the extemporaneous speaking competition," I offered.

"Deron, so did I!"

The two of us stared at one another in baffled amazement as I said aloud what we both were thinking: "That means we were in the same city, at the same event, and likely in the same room together two full years before we met in college. How is it that we've never discovered this before now?"

The truth is this: no matter how intimately you know a person, there is always more to learn. Intimacy requires an attitude of curiosity and an appetite for deeper discovery.

If you are married, travel back to the time you met your future spouse. Remember how you wanted to know everything about them? You loved to hear their stories and learn about the details of their past. If your curiosity for your spouse has diminished, what has changed? You did. Sometimes we tend to lose our taste for discovery.

Our capacity for intimacy was not lost in the fall, but it was severely damaged. But for a sweet pure moment, Adam and Eve were naked. They felt no shame. Their full disclosure to one another deepened with each passing day. Adam was nothing more than shaped sod. But Eve saw a sculpture that bore the fresh fingerprints of the Creator. Eve was built using secondhand parts. But Adam's eye was trained to notice she, too, was crafted with a skillful hand for a life-giving purpose.

Both saw in one another the artistic expression of the Master Creator. Though the same, they were different. Though separate, they were connected in a way words could not fully explain. They were each made by God and for one another.

Henri Rousseau, the nineteenth-century painter, was largely unappreciated during his lifetime. Pablo Picasso, however, recognized him as a genius. In 1908, Picasso was walking through an open-air market in Paris when he spotted a secondhand canvas in the cluttered back corner of a junk shop. His trained eye recognized the style, the brushstrokes, and the technique. He knew it was a Rousseau. What others mistook for junk, Picasso recognized as a masterpiece. Once the painting was purchased, he threw a party in honor of his find.[1]

Adam and Eve saw each other as a gift. They were each a magnum opus of the Master of the universe. Having each other was worth celebrating.

Is this application only a marriage thing? By no means!

Every day we walk past masterpieces. The person at the office? They bear the brushstrokes of genius. The waitress at your favorite breakfast spot? She is a one-of-a-kind expression of the ever-existing God. The seemingly ordinary people who live under your roof? They each bear the mark of the Master! At issue is not the worth of the people around us. The challenge is our ability to recognize the worth of all people and for our eyes to agree with reality as God sees it.

THE NAKED TRUTH

How then did nakedness move from virtue to vice? What changed for the first two humans that they no longer wished to be seen as they were originally created?

Here again, we meet with the full consequence of sin. Sin is more than bending the rules. Sin is breaking relationship.

I experienced my own sin-in-the-garden moment growing up. I lied to my father. He had taught me that truth was my friend and that lying was unacceptable. This all sounded fine and good until I had something to hide. The details of my lie are unimportant (and embarrassing). Let's just say, I was quick to craft my explanation and alibi. I impressed myself with how easily I manufactured my false account. The lie was told. The truth was concealed. Chances that the matter would ever come up again were slim. But something inside me was not right. I was unprepared for my inner emotions of guilt and shame. Of course, I was too young to put labels on my feelings. All I knew is I felt bad, and I wanted it to stop.

Almost against my will, my feet carried me into the presence of my father. I stood before him as my quivering voice owned the truth of my lie. Did my father forgive me? Yes. Did he still love me? Certainly. In fact, he told me so. But something changed in our relationship. Up to that moment, my father had never expressed disappointment in me. Now he did. Most stinging was the realization that the damaged relationship was my doing completely, and it couldn't be undone.

Now that I am older, I better understand my first experience with guilt and shame. I was guilty for having damaged my relationship with my father. I was ashamed because I had become exactly what my father did not want me to become—a liar. Guilt results from wrong action. Shame is the awareness of a flawed character. No doubt, Adam and Eve felt both. They bent the rules. But they broke the relationship—with the only Father they had ever known.

To make matters worse, their relationship with God was not the only relationship that took heavy damage. Their trust in one another was also tainted. Before the moment of sin, they could think each other's thoughts and trust each other's intentions. Now they were unsure and insecure. Ease had vanished, and in its place was awkwardness.

I must risk sounding overly theological to make an important point. Theologians have given a label to the way that sin taints every area of life. The phrase is *total depravity*. Simply put, total depravity is the belief (and truth) that sin doesn't know where to stop. Sin sticks to anything and everything it touches.

Adam and Eve did not intend to destroy their relationship with God. Sin, having done this, couldn't be contained. The duo's intimacy with each other was also tainted. And sin didn't stop there either. Adam's relationship to his work and Eve's relationship to her future were also sullied.

Examine your own life. Try to identify a single area of life that sin has left unaffected. Have you ever experienced a frustrating day? That's because sin has left you to live in a broken world. Your plans for a productive day at work are thwarted by unforeseen difficulties. Angered by your experience, you take your bitterness home and take it out on your spouse. Worried and angered over your now-difficult relationship, you lose sleep. Exhaustion exacerbates your downward spiral. Try as you may, you cannot seem to stop sin from sticking to every area of life. It's maddening that the more you try to contain it, the more sin manages to stick itself to the people and situations you hold most dear.

If we can't fix it, what do we do?

When we are guilty, the human instinct is to hide. It still happens when cameras record an arrested criminal being escorted into a jail. Almost without thinking, the criminal cups his hands over his face in a futile attempt to hide from a watching world.

Years ago, my family visited a remote Greek island. We chose a "family-friendly" beach, given our children were very young. But it seems the Greek definition of family-friendly differs significantly from the American understanding of the term. The first morning on the beach was an eye-opener, especially for our children.

My wife and I learned several lessons during our Mediterranean adventure. First, we learned to take great care when taking pictures. Attention was needed to the foreground *and* who or what might be lurking in the background. A cute shot of our sandcastle-building children could be ruined by a granny showing too much skin. Second, we learned children are far more resilient than adults. While my wife and I continued to experience discomfort from the over exposed people around us, our children adjusted to their new surroundings in a matter of hours.

But the most important lesson of all? Human nudity is not all it's cracked up to be. People aren't pretty. In no way do I mean to diminish the fact that we are sculpted by a loving and creative God. But I can't help but think that, much as many parents see their children, we have faces and bodies that only God our Father can love unconditionally, especially as life takes its toll. Clothes cover up our countless scars and flaws and bulges. The perfectly proportioned body exists only for a few and then usually as a result of intense maintenance. Perfection is fleeting and quickly fades. The truth remains that for the most part clothes are a blessing!

And how exactly did Adam and Eve attempt to cover their guilt and hide their shame? How did they clothe themselves? The Bible tells us they chose fig leaves for their garments. On the upside, fig leaves are among the largest leaves in that part of the world. Maximum surface area is good! But on the downside, once plucked, fig leaves quickly become brittle. Fig leaves conceal, but they are far from comfortable.

Adam and Eve chafed beneath their choice of clothing—a moment-by-moment reminder of the price of guilt and shame.

Consider how we have learned to cover over our own inferiority and flaws. Sometimes we use clothes to do so. Could it be that the most fashionable people are the most fearful? Keeping up with the trends may be the way a person copes with the secret fears of not feeling worthy of other's admiration. Certainly, there are those who genuinely love the pursuit of style for its own sake. But might it be that a slave to fashion has never experienced the freedom of being their true selves without the labels?

And our tendency to cover up goes beyond clothes. In the American culture, cars have become an extension of our identity. Job titles and top salaries serve the same purpose. Office manager is a step up from secretary. The CEO's salary is envied more than the janitor's wages. (I know, because I have held both jobs.) I would be lying if I didn't admit "lead pastor" has a certain confidence-inducing ring to it. Living in the right neighborhood, eating at the right restaurants, and presenting a well-curated online identity are all modern replicas of the feeble fig leaves once worn in the garden.

The cover-up continues! Guilt and shame are real and ravaging to our peace of mind. We chafe at the time, energy, and money we expend to ensure others see us for who we wish we truly were.

From time to time, I half-jokingly propose a special Sunday event for our church. I suggest that people roll out of bed on the morning of worship, get immediately in their cars, and drive to church. No makeup, no styled hair, no brushed teeth. At long last, we would indeed come to worship just as we are. But I know if I were to make good on this idea, it would certainly result in a low-attendance Sunday. Why? Because we hold dear the impression others have of us—even if it means foregoing the opportunity to be in the presence of God.

This need to cover up nearly cost me my career as a pastor. I wasn't hiding a secret sin. Nor was I living a double life. Somehow I had convinced myself that pastors must portray a certain persona. Years of wearing a smile when I was not in a smiling mood, years of taking on one more obligation when my calendar was full and my tank was empty, and years of allowing people to unload their negativity on me without feeling the freedom to share my honest perspective for fear of offending had worn me thin. My manufactured persona was concealing my true personality. It took several months of conversations from an experienced and gifted counselor to see what I was doing and to learn how to address my problem. At issue was not my chosen career, but how I was choosing to live because of my career.

In the end, we do well to acknowledge the naked truth of who we are and who we are not. Life is best lived within the reality of being who God created us to be rather than who others expect us to be. Søren Kierkegaard's famous line says it best: "Now with God's help I shall become myself."[2]

BAD WEATHER, WRONG CLOTHES

"Then the man and his wife heard the sound of the Lord God walking in the garden at the time of the evening breeze, and they hid from the Lord God among the trees of the garden," (Genesis 3:8). The older King James Version of the Bible refers to the evening breeze as "the cool of the day." Sounds serene, doesn't it? But who runs from a draft of air? It is more accurate to imagine the wind picking up. John Walton, an expert on the ancient cultural understandings behind the book of Genesis, says, "The resulting interpretation is that Adam and Eve heard the (terrifying) sound of God going through the garden with a storm wind. If so, then God is coming in judgment rather than for a daily conversation, which explains Adam and Eve's desire to hide."[3]

Growing up in the western reaches of Texas, I've seen my fair share of storms. I have even survived a tornado or two. The first was when I was six years old. To this day I remember the wall of sound generated by the wind.

As God moves toward Adam and Eve in the garden, the wind whips up. A little breeze? Hardly. A sudden and sustained gust that forces Adam and Eve to seek shelter? That's more like it. God storms into the garden, but don't think he's lost control. Humanity has lost its bearings, not God.

God asks Adam and Eve several pointed questions as a way of getting to the bottom of what they had done. Perhaps, in some ways, God still asks these questions today:

- *Where are you?* (Genesis 3:9)
- *Who told you that you were naked?* (Genesis 3:11)
- *Did you eat from the tree that I commanded you not to eat from?* (Genesis 3:11)

Where are you?

We hide. God searches for us. In fact, God will *never* cease his search. Few people have captured this truth better than Francis Thompson:

> I fled Him, down the nights and down the days;
> I fled Him, down the arches of the years;
> I fled Him, down the labyrinthine ways
> Of my own mind; and in the midst of tears
> I hid from Him, and under running laughter.[4]

Thompson's lengthy poem—"The Hound of Heaven"—acknowledges God's Eden-like bent to come after us even as we try to blend into the scenery. Hiding from God is as effective as a child covering her own eyes thinking she has made herself invisible to her parent. No matter how tight we close our eyes to God's existence and affection, he persists in his search until we give up our hiding ways.

Who told you that you were naked?

I think it is a fair interpretation of this question to read it like this: *Why are you letting other voices besides mine define who you are? Why can't you listen only to me?*

How might our lives look if we listened to God—and only God—to understand our true selves? But the fact is we crave the approval of others. Our need to belong overpowers the gift of being who we are created to be. It is never too late to change course. This becoming ourselves begins with hearing God's voice and stepping out from behind the image we have crafted to impress others. This is not self-help or self-improvement but a deeply spiritual surrender to our true personality.

Did you eat from the tree that I commanded you not to eat from?

The short answer is yes. But Adam and Eve hemmed and hawed while awkwardly scratching the itch created by their ever-stiffening fig leaves. Their excuses prove as ill-fitting as their choice of clothes.

Adam offers, "Well, God, the woman *you* made—and that I never asked for in the first place—fed me the fruit. Technically, I am not the one who ate from the tree."

Eve chimes in: "The snake *you* let in the garden caused me to be confused. May I enter a plea of insanity?"

Satan seems to be the only one to take full responsibility. In fact, he is proud of what he has accomplished.

God is merciful. He allows the first couple to confess. God is also gracious as he removes their brittle garments and replaces them with something far better suited to their needs. Even as God states the consequences, the Hound of Heaven is already in pursuit of his people. As God gifts the skins of animals to Adam and Eve, we pick up on a slight hint of the system of animal sacrifice we see later throughout the Older Testament. The only way for an animal to surrender its skin is to sacrifice its life. Innocent blood was needed to cover up the guilt and shame of the people who strayed from God.

But soon enough, God would go beyond giving animal skins to offering the skin of his son. The very fabric God would offer to cover our nakedness was already being woven in the loom of his mind.

THE KING'S CLOTHES

Jesus died naked. "Then they crucified him and divided his clothes, casting lots for them to decide what each would get," (Mark 15:24). Forget the mental image of a loin cloth strategically draped across the midriff of Jesus as he hangs from the cross. This cloth, found in most modern depictions of the crucifixion, was placed there for our comfort, not for historical accuracy. The Persians developed crucifixion, but the Romans perfected it. They learned with gruesome precision how to take the human body to its furthest-most point of pain and suspend it there for the longest amount of time. When death feels like a gift, torture has accomplished its purpose.

Add to the injury of crucifixion, the insult of nakedness. And why not? In Jesus's case it made sense. What better way to expose a criminal who fancied himself king than to uncover every part of his beaten, suffering, perspiring, and expiring body?

But what the Romans meant for shame, we see in a different way. Pilate and his guards unwittingly unveiled the purest picture of God's love ever witnessed by human eyes. We see it all! God's naked love for humanity. The depths of divine love lay bare.

Nakedness was initially a gift. Sin made nakedness a source of embarrassment. But now it has become a gift again in the form of a naked Savior who exposes the full extent of God's love for people.

God was naked and he felt no shame.

In much the same way God offered the skin of animals to the guilty pair, so he invites each of us to be clothed in Christ. "For those of you who were baptized into Christ have been clothed with Christ," (Galatians 3:27).

The Christians of the first century typically celebrated baptism only on Easter. As newly minted believers emerged naked from the water, they were dried and presented with a new set of clothes to commemorate the occasion. Their old dirty clothes, like their past lives, were dropped at the water's edge and forever left behind. The new garments symbolized the beginnings of a new person fully clothed in Christ. True, it takes time to understand the full extent of the new gift of being clothed in Christ, but we are clothed nonetheless as undeserving people receiving the unmerited grace of God.

Fellow pastor Rankin Wilbourne helps us use our imagination to better understand this idea:

> Imagine a little boy wearing his father's dress shirt. He is already fully clothed, you could say, but he's still just a little boy. He'll have to grow up into this new covering until it fits him. In the same way, we are already completely clothed in Christ and his

righteousness, but life in Christ is one of growing up into this new reality until it fits us. You are not striving to attain it. You are striving to lay hold of what is already yours. You are growing up into it.[5]

Louis Braille is a name familiar to most people. At the age of three he accidentally jabbed one of his father's tools—a stitching awl used for saddle making—into his eye. The sympathetic nerve connecting his eyes then rendered his good eye helpless. By the age of fifteen, Braille was already developing an alphabet for the blind by producing a series of raised dots on paper. It is ironic that he used a stitching awl to make his first letters. The tool that blinded him was the very tool that enabled him, and many others to follow, to experience the larger world of reading.[6]

We were rendered naked and afraid. And what does a naked sinner need? A naked Savior. Ironic, don't you think? We are clothed by the self-revealing, self-sharing, hold-nothing-back love of God.

TALK TO GOD

Lord God,
You know all my self-made hiding places.
My camouflaged personality proves poor protection from the cold.
Without you I am exposed and vulnerable.

Christ, clothe me!
Once bare and barely alive, I am humbled by your lifesaving love.
Shame is a thing of my past.
Amen.

TALK TO ONE ANOTHER

1. Is nakedness a good representation of innocence? What actually changed for Adam and Eve that led them to clothe themselves?

2. Modesty is a rather unpopular virtue today. Why does modesty often get thought of as prudish or old-fashioned?

3. Adam and Eve tried to hide from God after they sinned. How do you hide from God or other people? How do you try to clothe yourself to avoid exposure?

LISTEN TO SCRIPTURE

Job 1:20–21
Ecclesiastes 5:15
Revelation 3:17–19

TEN

And he said, "I heard you in the garden,
and I was afraid because I was naked, so I hid."

GENESIS 3:10

What would my life be like if I weren't afraid?

JAN JOHNSON, TWENTY-FIRST-CENTURY
SPIRITUAL FORMATION AUTHOR

What scares you?

It has been noted that a man keeps in the bottom right-hand drawer of his desk what he values and fears the most.[1] I wonder if this is true of you. It is for me. The bottom right-hand drawer of my desk contains my speaking material. Even after twenty-five years of speaking, it still takes a toll on my nervous system. I value and fear speaking in front of others.

What's in the bottom right-hand drawer of your desk?

Now let's go deeper. What do you keep in the bottom right-hand drawer of your mind? Deep down, what do you value and fear? A relationship? Your reputation? Your health or security? Reach deep into the back of this mental drawer. Is there something you keep hidden from even yourself?

What scares you?

BE AFRAID, BE VERY AFRAID

Fear is mentioned hard on the heels of humanity's first experience with sin. Adam and Eve had done the opposite of what God commanded. Satan slithered from the scene in silent triumph. God showed up and called out to his people. Suddenly, the first family was overwhelmed by an unexpected emotion. Attempting to put words to this new sensation, Adam says, "God. I. Am. Afraid. Of. You." Adam's trembling words form what could be considered the first prayer of the Bible. Overall, it's not a great prayer, but at least it's honest.

When afraid, humans instinctively respond in one of three ways.

First, we freeze. I experienced this for myself the night my oldest child came into the world. I had seen first-time fathers-to-be parodied on television and in movies. The moment the woman starts into labor, the husband loses his mind. I promised myself this would not happen to me. It did. My wife ordered me to find my car keys. *What are keys? What is a car?* My confusion, though short-lived, was proof that I am human despite my best efforts to prove otherwise. Simply put, I froze.

Second, anxiety may spark the desire to fight. Recently, I was at a hockey game. No sooner had the puck dropped did the two players in the face-off toss aside their sticks and gloves and began throwing fists at one another. Obviously, there was unfinished business from a previous game. While fighting makes for brilliant hockey, it proves a poor way to live. Might much of the anger we see in our world today—from road rage to online rants—be the result of the simple fact that people are afraid? We are afraid of not getting our way. We are afraid of what others will do to us if we don't strike first. We are afraid of losing an argument and losing face.

Finally, panic produces the impulse to flee. We run. If we feel like our problems won't disappear, we decide to make ourselves disappear. Don't you feel this in the moment when you are in conflict with another person? At such moments, we would rather be anywhere else than where we are. We want to run and hide until the problem goes away. Funny how it never does.

And this is exactly what Adam and Eve decide to do—flee. Being rookies at sin and inexperienced with fear, they hadn't yet learned the impossibility of fleeing beyond God's ability to find them. Psalm 139, had it been written at the time, would have told them the truth.

Where can I go to escape your Spirit?
Where can I flee from your presence?
If I go up to heaven, you are there;
if I make my bed in Sheol, you are there.
If I live at the eastern horizon
or settle at the western limits,
even there your hand will lead me;
your right hand will hold on to me.
—Psalm 139:7–10

What makes you afraid?

Or to ask the same question in a few different ways: What causes you to freeze? What makes you want to fight? Who or what are you running from?

AFRAID OF MY OWN SHADOW

Theologians tell us that when sin invaded the human condition we became forever estranged from four things. Could these four things be the very things we are most afraid of? Understanding these four categories will not necessarily ease our anxiety, but at least we will have a framework to grasp what before has been only nameless, nebulous fears. For humanity as a whole, this is what lurks in our collective bottom right-hand drawer.

We fear circumstances. When my children were younger, I was afraid they might drown. Since I nearly drowned as a child, my mind found it easy to fixate on this fear for the sake of my children. Any time my children were near water, I was on high alert. As my kids got older and swimming lessons accomplished their purpose, my fears eased. But they have never completely gone away.

Then my children began driving. They stayed out later and traveled farther from home. What I feared for my children around water, my wife feared for them while on the road. Whenever they are on the highway traveling to or from university, I know my wife will be tense until they have safely arrived.

My wife and I fear the same thing. The details of swimming or driving are secondary. We both fear circumstances beyond our control. Indeed, the less control we feel, the greater our anxiety. Learning to trust God when life is out of our control is a steep and lifelong learning curve.

We fear other people. People cannot be controlled any more than the circumstances around us. And what is it we fear? For the most part, we live in fear of losing people's approval or earning their disapproval. Early on we learn to operate for our parents' approval. Indeed, some people never outgrow this need. One middle-aged man confessed to me that he will be relieved on the day his father dies because he will finally have the freedom to become the man he wants to be unburdened from the potential of his father's criticism.

Our fear of other people goes beyond our family. We fear the opinions of the people watching our social media accounts. (We may even fear no one is watching us at all.) We fear the supervisor at work who isn't concerned with our longevity or happiness. We are afraid of finding no one to love us, leaving us to spend our life alone.

We are afraid of ourselves. How is this possible? How can we be afraid of who we are? Pay close attention to your thoughts. Have you ever caught your self-talk saying things such as, *Why do I always mess things up especially when things are going good?* or *Why do I always cause problems?* or *Why can't I ever do things right?* All people, some more than others, wrestle with self-criticism and self-doubt.

Our self-talk can create self-inflicted wounds, or our self-talk can become a source of self-administered healing. The choice is ours. Take for example a situation that does not go our way. We wound ourselves when we say, "I am a loser." However, the process of healing begins when we say, "I may have lost, but that does not change the fact that I will try again, only this time wiser."

Perhaps we choose self-wounding because it is easier. Or maybe we believe self-inflicted wounds are a form of penance for our mistakes. Whatever the reason, the results are the same: we fear the negativity of our own making.

We are afraid of God. This is the most damaging anxiety of all. Without God, we lack the courage to address the fear of our circumstances, other people, and ourselves. Faith in God is the cure for all other fears, but without God the disease will spread unchecked and incurable.

Don't make the mistake of thinking only non-Christians suffer from being afraid of God. Many longtime Jesus-followers find themselves struggling with this same overwhelming emotion. In my first book, I related a powerful moment while teaching at a children's camp. My message to the five-hundred-plus squirming children was this: God is not mean. As soon as I said these words, the room became completely still. I felt like Jesus's disciples on the stormy sea of Galilee as it was unexpectedly rendered silent. For the moment, the preteen tempest was quiet as they heard this good news.

Too many Christians grow up with the notion that God is angry at all times and for any number of reasons. Some inherit this God-view from ill-trained pastors or manipulative parents who threatened hell as the consequence of disobeying certain strict (and oftentimes silly) prohibitions. Tragically, their young psyches absorb the false notion that God does not want our adoration; he would rather we be afraid of him.

Over the years, I have counseled a number of adults who fear they have somehow managed to commit the unforgiveable sin. Is there such a thing as an unforgivable sin? Certainly. Jesus taught as much. A full discussion of this sin is best left for another time. For now consider one question: Why is there no pardon available for the unpardonable sin, whatever it might be? I have concluded that what qualifies the unforgivable sin as unforgivable is not the details of the transgression itself but the refusal on the part of the person committing it to ask God for the pardon only he can give. In other words, the fear of having committed the unforgivable sin contains the very proof of not having committed it in the first place!

In my pastoral work, I have also encountered people who grow increasingly afraid of God as they near life's end. I have counseled in the hospital rooms of people preparing to step into eternity. Death is in many ways the ultimate test of our faith. We must trust the goodness of God when the events in front of us do not seem to be good at all. God is the giver of life, but at the moment death seems to be stripping us of everything we hold dear. Our temporal doubts expose eternal questions. I have heard several people at such a moment say, "I hope I have been good enough for God to accept me into heaven." I try to be both firm and gentle at such moments. "Put your fears to rest," I say. "If you fear you have not done enough to deserve heaven, you are exactly right! But remember, this has never been the basis of your relationship with God. Remember that your trust is not in what you have done but in what Christ has done for you." Typically the switch of recognition flips on and their dark fears subside in light of the truly good news of the gospel.

NOTHING TO FEAR BUT FEAR ITSELF

Telling someone to not be afraid of God is a fool's errand. A simple illustration might help. Imagine someone telling you to not think about a pink elephant. What will happen? A pastel pachyderm will jump to the front of the mind. Told not to think about it, you will find it impossible to think about anything else. The secret to controlling our thoughts, as with many things we must learn how to control in life, is to replace an unwanted idea with a better one. If I begin to describe a sunny day with its flowers and fresh air, it won't be long before the pink elephant is forgotten.

In the same way, being afraid of God will not ease its grip on our hearts by direct willpower alone. Instead, we must indirectly conquer being afraid by replacing it with something far better—the fear of the Lord. This is more than a crafty turn of phrase. The phrase *the fear of the Lord* is possibly the most misunderstood phrase in the Bible. But what we have missed or misunderstood holds our liberation from everything in life that makes us afraid.

For starters, consider the phrase itself: *the fear of the Lord.* It is a compound phrase. Consider the way that compound words work. Two words are joined together forming an entirely different meaning than either one of the original words. Butterfly is not a stick of butter that flies. A cowboy is not a genetic hybrid between a child and a farm animal. An armpit is not a pit that holds extra arms. These examples, while silly, make my point. Meanings change when words are compounded. The same is true of this compound phrase—*the fear of the Lord.* It means something radically different than being afraid of God.

I do not claim to possess a perfect understanding of this idea, but whenever I encounter this phrase in the pages of the Bible, I replace it with a simple expression: *overwhelming wonder at the grandeur and grace of God.*

When I was six years old I survived my first tornado. Ingrained on my six-year-old mind are several indelible memories. I remember the sheer volume of the storm. I recall the total darkness of the house when the electricity failed. I recollect taking refuge on the orange couch in our living room. But most of all, I vividly remember not being afraid—at all. My six-year-old heart believed my mother and father would protect me. They had always protected me in the past, and this storm was no different. I was yet too young to understand that some things are more powerful than a loving parent's ability to protect. My thought was noble but misguided.

Now that I am much older, I tend to make the opposite mistake. My six-year-old mind overestimated my parents' power. My now-more-mature mind often underestimates God's power over circumstances well within his ability to handle. Most of my days are lived in a swirl of events beyond my ability to predict or control. But God's grandeur is stronger than any force I will face. God's grace is more powerful than any problem I will ever encounter. In short, God's goodness outpaces the evil that pursues me. As life happens around me and to me, I can choose to be overwhelmed by life, or I can choose to live in the fear of the Lord—overwhelmed by God's grandeur and grace.

It is one thing to accept this fact with my mind. It is another to live out this truth from my heart. How can I ever truly stop being afraid of God and instead live in fear of the Lord?

Psalm 19 explores two of the primary ways God reveals himself to his created people. The first is through nature.

The heavens declare the glory of God,
and the expanse proclaims the work of his hands.
—Psalm 19:1

Nature speaks to God's existence. But the natural world fails to accurately reveal the nature of the God who exists. A thunderstorm may tell one person that God is a God of power, while the same storm might convince another that God is a God of anger. Trying to pin down God's character from nature alone is not easy, nor will it ease our tendency to be afraid of him.

This is why God reveals himself in a second and more specific way:

The instruction of the LORD is perfect,
renewing one's life;
the testimony of the LORD is trustworthy,
making the inexperienced wise.
The precepts of the LORD are right,
making the heart glad;
the command of the LORD is radiant,
making the eyes light up.
The fear of the LORD is pure,
enduring forever;
the ordinances of the LORD are reliable
and altogether righteous.
—Psalm 19:7–9 (emphasis mine)

God's grandeur and grace are secrets hidden in plain sight. In his grandeur, God created us to share in the joy of his created order. In his grace, God reveals to us that the best way for us to live is at the center of his existence.

The fear of the Lord fundamentally changes the way we understand and experience the commands of God. Now even God's laws are expressions of his grace. Consider the simple command that prohibits coveting. Coveting is the internal desire for more—a desire often informed by what other people have that we do not. What a miserable way to live! To covet is to be held captive by everything we do not yet possess. How gracious of God to reveal that we have a choice in this matter. As an alternative, he commands we develop the habit of contentment. We can be free from being possessed by possessions. We can appreciate an object without having to own it ourselves. We can even celebrate that God has seen fit to not entrust certain objects to our care. I can rest in the joy that God provides all I need, not necessarily all I want.

Sexual promiscuity is another obvious example. Imagine a couple spending a lifetime together, relishing the seasons of plenty and weathering the seasons of want. Sitting with each another at a fiftieth anniversary, they will likely experience an ecstasy of intimacy to which a thousand one-night stands cannot begin to compare. God's ways are good. God's ways are best.

Bible scholar Robert Pratt tells of a time in college when he visited his on-campus chapel. At the front of the chapel stood a traditional stained glass window. The sun outside and the stained glass in the chapel conspired to play tricks on his eyes. When the sun was behind the clouds, the window behaved much like a mirror. Pratt could see his own reflection. When the sun emerged, Pratt's vision shifted to see the grass outside through the clearer panes of glass. Finally, as Pratt walked out of the chapel, he looked back. Now he was able to see the stained glass in its entirety and the full picture it presented. The stained glass, under certain circumstances, behaved as a mirror, a window, and a picture.[2]

The Bible serves us in much the same way. At times, the Bible serves as a mirror allowing us to see ourselves more clearly—sinful condition and all. At other times, the Bible serves as a window enabling us to understand the reality of the world as it is. Not least, the Bible is a picture, giving us as much of a full understanding of God as our minds and souls can contain.

Life is big, but God is greater. Life is hard, but God gives the grace to face it. No longer need we live in the grip of anxiety. Other people are put in their proper places of influence, our circumstances are put in perspective, and our view of our self is rightsized because we have a reference point beyond our own fickle feelings. God is bigger than all these forces put together, and his graciousness goes beyond our wildest dreams.

Proverbs 9:10 says, "The fear of the LORD is the beginning of wisdom, and the knowledge of the Holy One is understanding." When we get life right, we have God to thank for it. And when we lack perfection, God is patient. Indeed, it is through the greatest failures of life that God will teach the most lasting lessons. If you know someone of great wisdom, chances are this person earned their wisdom the hard way—through tedious trial and ample error.

Henri Nouwen was a Catholic priest. Having visited a circus, he became enthralled by the flying trapeze artists. He went so far as to befriend a family of trapeze artists known as The Flying Rodleighs.

One day, I was sitting with Rodleigh, the leader of the troupe,

> in his caravan, talking about flying. He said, "As a flyer, I must have complete trust in my catcher. The public might think that I am the great star of the trapeze, but the real star is Joe, my catcher. He has to be there for me with split-second precision and grab me out of the air as I come to him in the long jump.
>
> "How does it work?" I asked.
>
> "The secret," Rodleigh said, "is that the flyer does nothing and catcher does everything. When I fly to Joe, I have simply to stretch out my arms and hands and wait for him to catch me and pull me safely over the apron behind the catchbar."[3]

According to Rodleigh, the flyer must resist the temptation to catch the catcher. Broken bones and deadly falls will be the result. Instead, the flyer must resolve to do nothing but wait and allow himself to be caught. The catcher makes the effort; the flyer makes himself available. The catcher must develop disciplined timing; the flyer must master the art of trust.

God reveals to us the best way to live. We must not be afraid to launch our lives into the thin air of obedience. We must trust God will catch us. When we succeed, we experience, with precision, the timing that only the God of eternity controls. Afraid, we are weak. Living in fear of the Lord produces people of power.

DON'T WORRY, BE HAPPY

Acts 2 contains a famous snapshot of the early church. "Everyone was filled with awe, and many wonders and signs were being performed through the apostles," (Acts 2:43). The awe of God—the fear of the Lord—fueled the church's passionate worship, their authentic community, and their commitment to boldly proclaim the gospel. The church grows weak not for lack of effective programing or the latest tech or the trendiest worship fashions. The church loses true power when it loses its sense of the fear of the Lord. Without the fear of the Lord, the body of Christ becomes a corpse in need of revival or burial.

What is true of the church is also true on the level of each individual Jesus-follower. Trifling with God results in a trivial life. Look around. See it for yourself. To live for the banalities of gossip and greed and small talk is to live a life void of boldness and meaning. But if we fear the Lord, we will live powerful lives, overwhelmed with the grandeur and grace of God and underwhelmed by any cheap substitute the world might offer.

I enjoy stories of people who discover who they truly are late in life. One such person was Edith Wilma Connor. In her sixties, she retired from her data entry job to become a competitive bodybuilder. At the age of seventy-seven, she was recognized by Guinness as the oldest female bodybuilder in the world.[4]

Barbara Hillary, a retired nurse, discovered that no African American woman had ever trekked to the North Pole. She decided to do so herself. Add to her feat the fact that lung cancer had deprived her of one-quarter of her breathing capacity, and her accomplishment takes on even greater meaning. She went on to visit the South Pole, becoming the only African American female to tag both poles.[5]

Emma Gatewood. This sixty-seven-year-old grandmother of twenty-three became the first woman to solo the Appalachian Trail. Her 146-day journey over 2,050 miles cost her six pairs of shoes.[6]

These accounts remind us we are never too old to become who we know we should have been all along—people living the adventure of life and in fear of the Lord.

Being afraid of God makes us smaller. But the fear of the Lord enlarges our souls beyond our own expectations. Afraid of God we will live at an uncomfortable distance from him. It is in the fear of the Lord that we find the intimacy we crave. Afraid of God is to live a life of running. The fear of the Lord means walking each day with our God from now into eternity.

TALK TO GOD

Lord God,
I am afraid of many things—at times even you.
I am tired of my trepidations and hesitations,
My angst, anxiety, and overreactions.

Take hold of me—that which I can change,
As well as all that is outside my control.
Keep both in your steady hands.
Amen.

TALK TO ONE ANOTHER

1. Why is fear often presented as contrary to faith in the Bible? How does fear indicate lack of trust in God?

2. In John 14:27, Jesus tells his disciples he is leaving them with peace instead of fear. How does Jesus help you be at peace instead of fearful?

3. First John 4:16–21 says there is no fear in love. Is this really true? Why? How does love drive out fear?

LISTEN TO SCRIPTURE

Genesis 15:1

Psalm 31:11–16

Matthew 6:25–34

Luke 12:4–7

ELEVEN

You will eat bread by the sweat of your brow . . .

GENESIS 3:19

The more you sweat in peace,
the less you bleed in war.

NORMAN SCHWARZKOPF, TWENTIETH-CENTURY AMERICAN GENERAL, QUOTING AN ANCIENT CHINESE PROVERB

What happens at the exact moment we die? What will we experience in our final instant as we move from this life to the next?

Researchers at Jerusalem's Hadassah University interviewed 271 people who had experienced a near-death event and had lived to tell about it. Those interviewed recounted what researchers call a Life Review Experience or LRE. In layman's terms, their life flashed before their eyes. During an LRE, people lost all sense of time as the meaningful and memorable moments of their life played out in front of them. These scenes were not necessarily in chronological order; in fact, some scenes played out simultaneously. Most of the people interviewed credited their LRE as an event that transformed their perspective on life.

Researchers discovered that the last area of the brain to shut down during death is the region of the brain responsible for our autobiographical information. It seems that as a person approaches death, God gives us one final gift—the ability to see all of our life in one single frame.[1]

But is there a way to see our lives from this powerful perspective without the inconvenience of dying? What impact might we experience if we could behold all of our life—both the temporal and the eternal—as one comprehensive and clear picture?

NO SWEAT

Let's begin with the truth that life is a gift. Remember that we have already explored the fact that other ancient cultures besides the Hebrews had their own explanation for the origins of life. Most all of these creation stories are rated R for violence. For instance, a group of gods grew weary of the labor necessary for their level of divine existence. In their fatigue, these gods created and then outsourced these tedious tasks to the human race. Humans were born under the burden of meeting the gods' demands and satisfying their whims.

The Hebrew creation account turns such an idea completely on its head. The Bible tells us humans were not created to provide for God. Instead, when God placed people on the earth he did so with the intent of providing for us. Instead of humans providing goods to the gods, God supplies humans with all the good they would ever need.[2]

Life is a gift! Imagine a panorama of the Garden of Eden. God gives everything: food, sunlight, space, companionship, and clear commands. All of this (and more, I am sure) was no sweat for Adam and Eve. Without effort, they enjoyed the richness of God's world. Best of all, God gave himself to his creation. Adam and Eve had uninterrupted access to God himself. The joy of such a full existence is hard to fathom. But it's worth a try.

Consider for a moment that you are the only individual to ever exist who has had the privilege to be you. In all of history and throughout all eternity, you are the only person to bear your looks, your personality, and your perspective on the world. *You* are the only *you* that will ever exist. How is this not a gift? God has created everything on purpose and with a purpose, which includes you. Without you, the world would not become the world as God intends it to be.

When God created Adam, God gave Adam a clear instruction. Adam was not permitted to lounge about or lose himself in leisure. Adam was summoned to work and watch over all God had made. Perhaps God wanted Adam to expand the borders of the garden. God's design and man's desire together could conquer and craft the entire planet into perfection. Don't we still find within ourselves a strong desire to produce and to protect something of value for our world? This characteristic is lingering evidence that we are made to create something good from the world around us.

Consider the old story of three workmen on a building site. All three were laying brinks for a building that would become a cathedral. A visitor asked the first man, "What are you doing?"

"I am laying bricks."

The visitor asked the second bricklayer the same question.

"I am building a church."

The third man responded to the same question with a beaming face, "I am building a house for God."

The first man had a job. The second man had a career. The third man had a calling. The third man saw his life, his task, and God's world for the gifts they are. The bricklayer-builder, like Adam the gardener, was made to work and watch over all that God had given him as a simple way of honoring his Creator.

I regret that it took me so long to discover this truth. Once, in front of a group of leaders, I was explaining my choice of vocation as a pastor. I arrogantly stated that if I had not clearly sensed God's calling in this direction, then I would have been better off to sell insurance. No sooner had the words left my lips when I made eye contact with a good friend who works in the insurance industry. I saw his soul deflate as I compared my high calling to his mediocre existence. I later apologized privately.

Since that time, I have come to see a more biblical picture. No call of God is a trifling thing. Who am I to say that another person's vocation is of less worth for the simple fact that it is not my vocation? How might God use the avenue of insurance to meet practical needs and open the door for meeting spiritual needs? Indeed, my friend is working and watching over his slice of God's creation.

Every vocation matters. The very word *vocation* resembles the word *vocal.* In fact, they share the same root word *vocare*—a Latin word meaning "calling." God speaks. We listen. We experience through our giftedness the beauty of being ourselves.

And just how do we listen to God's callings? I suggest three things. First, we must listen to the passions God has put within us. Are you passionate about helping children or saving marriages or balancing numbers or helping people get in shape? These passions may be clues to your calling. Next, give attention to your natural abilities. What are the things you have a knack for that come so easy that you cannot fathom why others can't do the same thing? This is God gifting you with a unique ability to discipline to the height of usefulness. Finally, notice the opportunities God sends your way. If God wishes to use our passions and gifts, then he will certainly orchestrate avenues for our abilities to be utilized to their fullest.

Can you see it?

Life is a gift!

Enjoy your uniqueness. Relish in the God who gives good things to you and through you.

WORKING UP A SWEAT

Remember what we are trying to do—to see all of life in a single frame. So far, we have seen that life is a gift, but there is more to the picture than this. If we are to see the full and true picture, then we must embrace the reality that life is lived under a curse. Everything God originally intended for our lives has been frustrated and fragmented.

Worst of all, this curse is our own doing.

A single word in Genesis 3 captures the effect of all that is wrong with the world: "You will eat bread by the *sweat* of your brow" (Genesis 3:19, emphasis mine).

Sweat. Not a particularly beautiful word, is it?

No doubt you have sweated before. We sweat when we cook a meal in a hot kitchen and when we clean the stove afterward. We sweat while mowing the lawn or laying carpet or constructing an outbuilding.

I once uprooted a tree. The tree was all but dead. It was unsightly and needed replacing. Because I wanted to plant another tree in that exact spot, everything below ground needed to go. It was a small tree—or so I thought. It took several hours over several days and the help of a tenacious friend to finally free the root ball's hold from its piece of earth. I rarely see the new tree without remembering the sweat required to remove the old.

The mention of sweat in Genesis 3 represents more than the physical act of perspiring. Stress is now part of life's lot. Strain now stains the once pristine picture of the gift of life. Pain is a force from which not one of us is exempt. We lose sleep. We lose confidence. We lose patience. We lose peace. If we are not careful, we may lose hope. Life remains a gift, but now life is somehow tainted with a curse—the curse of a hard-labored existence. Every pleasure is tinged with pain.

Mel Blanc was the creator and voice actor for several of the cartoon characters many of us remember from our childhood. Bugs Bunny and Porky Pig are only two of the characters brought to life through his imagination and voice. His tombstone bears the inscription, "That's all folks"—a fitting epitaph for a man who spent his life entertaining others.

As the voice actor for Bugs Bunny, Blanc insisted on performing every noise coming from Bugs' mouth. Professional integrity demanded it. Blanc himself performed Bugs Bunny's signature chomping and chewing of carrots. But Mel Blanc hated the taste of carrots. He despised them, in fact. After each chomp and chew, the recording was paused while Blanc spit the spent carrots into a nearby waste can.[3] At the end of each recording session, a pile of carrot pulp bore silent witness to a simple truth: while Blanc loved his job, there was a part of it he had a hard time swallowing. Even producing something as innocent and fun as cartoons is not always easy or pleasant.

Isn't the same true for all of us? As much as we might enjoy our job, there are sure to be parts of it we dislike. The paperwork perhaps? A disagreeable client?

Marriage is a joy. But place two imperfect people under the same roof and you have the makings of the perfect storm.

Parenting is a pleasure. Then teenagers happen.

Life not only proves unpleasant, but it is frequently unproductive. I have friends in the oil industry who speak of drilling dry wells. Study, planning, money, and hundreds of sweat-equity hours are invested to drill where it is believed oil will be found. Then it is not. Losses are cut. Sites are abandoned. Fingers are pointed. And if it happens too many times, jobs are lost. In the back of our minds we know that life's road has its fair share of dead ends. Frustrating, isn't it?

Several months ago, I was stranded in a medium-sized city in a less-than-medium-sized airport. One restaurant and one shop were all I had for hours on end. My route home was blocked by weather. The counter agent was polite and helpful. She reassured me with the promise, "I will get you home tonight." True to her word, I stumbled in the door just before midnight. Promise kept. The next day, I called customer service for the airline. Airline personnel endure grief when things go badly even when they are not to blame. I felt the agent who had helped me deserved a kudo and the airline deserved a compliment for hiring her.

As I spoke with the customer service representative who took my call, she asked me to stop talking mid-story. Through her partially covered microphone, I could hear her ask her supervisor, "How do I fill out a compliment card?" How rare do compliments have to be before forgetting how to process one? Yet, this is the world we inhabit. Complaints are the order of the day. Compliments are few and far between.

Are you getting the picture? Like it or not, God's gift of life and the curse of sin occupy the same space in the single frame of our existence.

The gift of life evokes joy. The curse inspires complaint. This tug-of-war over our attitude is something we deal with our entire lives. Try as we may, we all have days when our attitude refuses to obey our desire to stay focused on gratitude for all God has given us.

Even Columbus, as he was discovering new worlds and a new worldview, dealt with the frustration of broken ships and halting progress. In his journal he summed up his response to the sweat of stress and shattered expectations like this: "I see that I'm going to have to accept what I cannot control."[4]

Life is a gift, but a broken one. We live in a world where every pleasure is tinged with pain and every stride of productivity is met by the stumble of frustration.

SWEAT EQUITY

Christy Brown was born with cerebral palsy in 1932. He was born with little more than the ability to move his left foot. Doctors told Christy's parents they should expect him to have little quality of life. They were encouraged to institutionalize their new son. But the parents refused, believing that there was more to Christy than met the eye.

One day, as Brown was lying on the floor of his home, one of his siblings dropped a crayon near his foot. Young Christy Brown stretched his foot and seized the crayon. He began to move and manipulate the crayon between his toes. A writer was born! With the help of specialized computers, Brown has written multiple books using only his mind and the big toe of his left foot.[5] There is something beautiful about perseverance. The decision to practice resilience despite obstacles often highlights what is most beautiful about the human spirit. Obstacles make achievement more stunning and awe-inspiring than it otherwise would have been. So what is your excuse for not getting on with your plans?

I hope you are seeing with greater clarity yet another layer of the single frame of life! Because life is a gift that has been cursed, we must become people of perseverance. Indeed, the people I most admire are those who make themselves responsible for pushing through the circumstances that might hold others back. We cannot always decide what happens to us. But we all have the ability to decide what happens within us as we face the gift-yet-curse of life.

We see perseverance time and again in Scripture, don't we? Elijah pressed on through his depression (1 Kings 19:10–18). Jeremiah remained true to his convictions even as he was labeled unpatriotic and heretical (Jeremiah 38:1–6). Nehemiah continued to rebuild the wall around Jerusalem even as people around him tried to tear him down (Nehemiah 4).

A nugget of wisdom to this effect is attributed to both Abraham Lincoln and Winston Churchill. It says this: "Success is going from failure to failure without losing your enthusiasm."[6] Perhaps Lincoln said it. Maybe it was Churchill. Perhaps neither said it. But both men embodied this truth in the way they practiced perseverance during their difficult times.

Even the disciples of Jesus each faced the challenge of remaining true to their Master as they experienced the inertia of a world moving away from God. That is why Jesus told them, "If the world hates you, understand that it hated me before it hated you," (John 15:18).

This quality of perseverance and resilience is to mark our character until our dying day. Could the curse of Genesis 3 also serve as a challenge to not drop out of the race of life until we have crossed our finish line? "You will eat bread by the sweat of your brow until you return to the ground" (Genesis 3:19).

We are given the gift of life. Lived under a curse, we persevere through our sweat. When the final ounce of sweat is wrung from our brow, we will fall as dry as dust in death.

BLOOD, SWEAT, AND TEARS

So is this our lot, to sweat to death?

The word *sweat*—at least in our English versions of the Bible—appears only twice as a noun in Scripture. The first is when Adam and Eve caused a curse to fall on God's gift of life. Exiled from Eden, they secured for themselves and their posterity lives of stress and strain. Perseverance was then required to meet and conquer life's challenges.

The only other time sweat appears in the Bible as a noun is in the pages of the New Testament. But unlike Adam and Eve who were expelled from a garden and condemned to a life of sweat, we see one man enter a garden and sweat it out on our behalf. It is Jesus.

Jesus had invested three years in a small band of men. He proclaimed the simple message that God is King. He pushed his followers to live within this life-changing and eternity-altering reality. Religious stress of Jewish opposition and political strain of Roman suspicion had reached their climax. Jesus comes to a garden to sweat it out. "Being in anguish, he prayed more fervently, and his sweat became like drops of blood falling to the ground," (Luke 22:44). What exactly did Jesus experience at this stressful moment?

William Edwards, decades ago, wrote a brilliant article for *The Journal of the American Medical Association.* Edwards detailed the physical effects of what Jesus suffered during his torture and trial. Even though it was written from a medical perspective, it is still readable to the nonmedical mind.

Edwards believes Jesus likely experienced a condition called hematidrosis. Hematidrosis occurs when severe stress causes the blood vessels adjoining the sweat glands to rupture. The blood evacuates the body through the skin pores. Jesus may have appeared to his disciples as though he was sweating blood.[7]

Or perhaps Jesus did not sweat blood at all. Perhaps he was sweating as one might bleed—profusely. We can't say for sure what Jesus was experiencing physically. But we know with certainty what Jesus felt emotionally. Jesus was under intense stress and immense strain. The word *anguish* is used here as Jesus endures the emotions of his approaching crucifixion. Jesus is stretched emotionally, spiritually, physically, and mentally. He was stretched almost to the breaking point.

Ductility is the word used to express how far a physical object can be stretched before it breaks. Some materials can be stretched more than others. Gold is among the most ductile of elements. A single ounce of gold can be stretched into a wire fifty miles long before breaking.[8] That's ductility! Jesus was a strong man. He proved himself flexible with the narrow-minded religious leaders and the overly proud political forces, and resilient toward the demands of needy followers pulling him in different directions. But here in the garden of Gethsemane, we see Jesus stretched to the point of breaking. This moment should give us pause to reflect deeply on the nature of Jesus and the near-breaking point he endured on our behalf.

Just as we are attempting to see all of our life in a single frame, it is worth the effort to behold as much as we can see of Jesus's life all at once.

Jesus's life is a gift to all of humanity. Jesus reveals God in ways never seen before. Thirty-five miracles in the Gospels bear testimony to the power of God flowing through his life. His healing miracles tell us God is stronger than our pain. His nature miracles reveal God is stronger than our surroundings. Jesus's ability to cast out demons reminds us God is stronger than any other spiritual force we might face. Three resuscitations—returning life to people who had died—tell us that God's power is stronger than death. Jesus's life is such a gift that he gives vitality to everyone he touches.

But Jesus allowed himself to fall under a curse—a curse that is rightly ours to bear. Jesus endured the cross, which Scripture confirms as a curse. As Deuteronomy 21:23 says, "For anyone hung on a tree is under God's curse." To the Romans, Jesus was a potential revolutionary to be executed. To the Jews, Jesus was a heretic to be exterminated. Both parties considered him cursed.

But Jesus perseveres. He does not give up until the last drop of life—blood, sweat, and tears—is surrendered on our behalf. Jesus has lived our lives. Gift. Curse. Perseverance. He has experienced every part of our reality. Now he invites us into the new reality of his resurrection. There is sweetness beyond the sweatiness of life as we know it. Beyond death, there is life like what we have never imagined.

The national arboretum in Washington, D.C., has many trees, but one particular tree bears special meaning. It is a bonsai tree given by the Japanese government to the United States in honor of the nation's 1976 bicentennial. The tree has a rich history. It was planted in 1625. In 1945, the bonsai tree stood within the two-mile blast radius of the atomic bomb dropped by the United States on Hiroshima. It survived only because it happened to be resting behind a wall that absorbed the brunt of the blast. This small tree tells a big story.[9]

There is another tree. It is ancient. Planted some two millennia ago at ground zero of humanity's sin, the person who occupied this tree absorbed the punishment that rightly belongs to us. The tree now stands as the tomb now sits—empty. Resurrection is our new and ultimate reality.

This is existence in a single frame.

Life is a gift.

We live and sweat under a curse.

Like Jesus, we persevere with the patience provided by God.

A new reality of eternity has been opened through the sweaty body of our Savior.

TALK TO GOD

Lord God,
Life is large, and my soul so small. The thorns of the field
And the thorns in my flesh intertwine, making life less livable.
Such strain and stress are my birthright to bear.

But Jesus, you chose to sweat it out with me
Better yet—for me.
Your touch reminds me I am never alone.
Amen.

TALK TO ONE ANOTHER

1. How do you cope with the pain, agony, and stress associated with your life? Do you tend to complain? Do you overwork? Do you self-medicate? Do you procrastinate?

2. What positive habits can you adopt to equip you to deal better with the stress and strain of life?

3. There is a popular expression "no pain, no gain." Why do you think God has established most progress to be mingled with pain?

LISTEN TO SCRIPTURE

Ecclesiastes 2:18–26
Matthew 20:1–16
Colossians 3:22–25

TWELVE

ONE FINAL, PERFECT WORD

In the beginning God created
the heavens and the earth.

GENESIS 1:1

In the beginning was the Word, and the Word
was with God, and the Word was God.

JOHN 1:1

Charles Dodgson was a professor of mathematics at Oxford University. He also had a talent for writing children's stories. We still celebrate his opus *Alice in Wonderland,* which he penned under the name Lewis Carroll.

When *Alice in Wonderland* was first released, Queen Victoria of England sent Dodgson a note saying she would be "pleased to accept any other works by the same pen." In reply, Dodgson sent the queen a copy of his only other published work—*Syllabus of Plane Algebraical Geometry.*[1]

We intuitively understand that some books are easier to read than others. The Bible feels more akin to Carroll's *Syllabus* than his *Alice.* With its 1,189 chapters and three-quarters of a million words, the Bible does not surrender itself to us without effort. When I first began to pursue God for myself, I instinctively went to the Bible for guidance. Not knowing where to start, I guessed. I found myself in Isaiah. Little did I know then that I was hardly the first person to be baffled by Isaiah's long-ago prophecies (Acts 8:30–34).

These days I spend the better part of my ministry as a pastor trying every way I know how to make Scripture more understandable. Sometimes I succeed. Many times I do not. For every minute I spend on a platform or behind a podium, I invest twenty minutes in preparation. I love the preparation, but at the same time, I dread it. When I study, I face my own lack of understanding and obedience. But when I persevere, I uncover for myself what I want my hearers to discover—

the unstoppable love of God. My hope has been to accomplish the same thing within the borders of this book.

Ten words have been our guide. Each word tells the story of the Bible in its own unique way. See how far we have traveled together:

Light—God's first creation. Light still dawns today on those who have eyes to see it.

Dust—We are made of gritty stuff. But God delights in our earthy ordinariness.

Breath—We are more than meets the eye. God delights in breathing fresh air and new life into our feeble frames.

Garden—God designed us to live close to his throne and close to his heart.

River—God's blessing is ours. We need only place ourselves within its flow.

Eat—The first command was not to eat. We failed. In response, Jesus gives us a final command to eat from the fruit of salvation found only in him.

Alone—Loneliness was never our destiny. God has given us other people. Better still, God has offered himself to us to satisfy our love starved souls.

Naked—We were once naked and ashamed. Jesus was unashamedly naked to reveal God's love to us.

Afraid—Fear is real. God is greater.

Sweat—Our curse is lifted by Christ. The sweat of our brow is relieved by the shedding of his blood.

My current favorite among this decalogue is *afraid*. I have lived many years in fear's shadows. But as I have gotten older, I have grown bolder. I have learned courage is not the absence of fear. Instead, courage is acting in a way that evokes fear. I am constantly relearning and remembering that being afraid is not what God originally intended for the human experience. Instead of being afraid of life, I choose to live in the fear of the Lord—forever overwhelmed with wonder at his grandeur and his graciousness.

STRONG WORDS

So, our ten words are now complete. However, I would be remiss if I did not offer one final word. This is not an eleventh word, mind you, but a word that stands over and above the others. In my estimation, this term captures the Bible in a single and glorious word. This word illuminates the other 749, 999 words found in Scripture. This word is a name—*Jesus.*

Frederick Buechner, in his usual way of saying things in an unusual fashion, pictured God as the bard of creation and Jesus as his perfect poem.

> God is poet, say, searching for the right word. Tries Noah, but Noah is a drinking man, and tries Abraham, but Abraham is a little too Mesopotamian with all those wives and whiskers. Tries Moses, but Moses himself is trying too hard; and David too handsome for his own good; Elisha, who sicks the bears on the children. Tries John the Baptist with his locusts and honey, who might also have worked except for something small but crucial like a sense of the ridiculous or a balanced diet.
>
> Word after word God tries and then finally tries once more to say it right, to get it all into one final Word what he is and what human is and why the suffering of love is precious and how the peace of God is a tiger in the blood.[2]

God refuses to remain silent. When he speaks, he expresses himself with perfection and precision. And his final word? Jesus.

Paul, in a letter to early Christians, ponders this mystery of God's ability to articulate himself. Though eternal and equal to God, Jesus did not exploit his uniqueness for his own convenience. Instead, Jesus embraced humility and sacrifice as the *modus operandi* of God's way to capture our attention and conquer our hearts.

> For this reason God highly exalted him
> and gave him the name
> that is above every name,
> so that at the name of Jesus
> every knee will bow—
> in heaven and on earth
> and under the earth—
> and every tongue will confess
> that Jesus Christ is Lord,
> to the glory of God the Father.
> —Philippians 2:9–11

There's that one word again: Jesus.

Every parent knows those moments when a child loses control. Temper tantrums are a part of parenting. It is not the parent's job to simply stop these outbursts of temper. The parent's true task is to teach their children how to avoid losing control in the first place. What do we say to our young charges? "Use your words! Don't resort to screams and tears. Words, not noise, are the best ways to communicate yourself." Indeed, a mark of maturity is the ability to express ourselves through words in such a way that reveals our mind so that we will be understood.

By this measure, God is the most mature being in the universe! He has compressed everything he desires to communicate of his loving mind and longing heart into a singularly profound word. Everything God wants us to understand and appreciate about him is summed up in a name—Jesus.

BIG WORDS

John, the fourth voice in the quartet of biblical writers who tell Jesus's story, opened his Gospel with an intentional echo of Genesis 1. Jesus's coming is best compared to creation itself. Jesus's arrival was nothing less than a new beginning, a starting over. Through him, God's creation was getting an opportunity for a fresh start. "In the beginning was the Word . . ." (John 1:1).

Why did John use "Word" to describe Jesus? Consider this: just as God inaugurated the first creation by using words, so he summoned his new creation into existence by the use of a single, significant Word. God has something to say to us through Jesus, and we would do well to listen.

Only two words come close to being understood by nearly every culture and language on the planet. The word *OK* is one of them. While etymologists debate *OK*'s origin, they agree upon its universality.

The other word is something we say when we are confused. The word is *Huh?* The possible exception to this is in the South. In Texas particularly, *Huh* is trumped by the earthier expression "Do what?" Yes, some things make sense only to insiders.

There may be other words that step with such ease across languages and cultures, but such words are few and far between.

In the ancient world to which John wrote his Gospel, the word *Word* crossed cultural boundaries with the same ease as *OK* and *huh*, at least with the two cultures in which Christianity was taking shape—Hebrew and Greek.

Word made immediate sense to Hebrew hearers. Those who grew up on the Jewish Scriptures instantly connected *Word* with the creation event. As we have explored time and again throughout this volume, God used his words to create reality as we know it. God spoke and things happened.

The Hebrew language has some ten thousand words total. Compared to English's 650,000 words, the Hebrew tally feels a bit light. But what Hebrew lacks in variety, it makes up for in ingenuity. Many Hebrew words pull double duty. The Hebrew word *debhar* (word) is a perfect example. *Debhar* can represent a spoken word. But *debhar* can also mean the event itself. Why is this significant?

Perhaps you know the expression "He is as good as his word." We admire people whom we trust so deeply that if they say they will do something, it is as good as done. No need to circle-back, follow-up, or check-in. When this type of person gives their word, we trust them to take the responsibility to make good on their promise.

When God said, "Let there be light," it was certain to happen. No doubts. No worries. No excuses. From the very first page, the Bible tells us God always makes good on his word. What he says, he will do.

Thus, John's opening scene takes us back to the threshold of creation where one of the most essential elements of God's character is first revealed—God's utter faithfulness. Just as God spoke his first creation into being, now he offers a new creation by speaking Jesus to our world.

One of the most memorable days of my life was a cold February morning in 1997—the day my daughter was born. When her head crowned, the doctor invited me to have a look. (My wife cringes every time I tell this story. It is only by her gracious consent that this account is included here.)

At first, I resisted the doctor's invitation. I wasn't sure if my stomach would be able to handle the sight. Thankfully he insisted. Not only did I see my daughter before her birth, but I also had the privilege of touching her head before she made her entrance into the world. Even today, when I pass my daughter as she sits on the couch or at the dinner table, I kiss her on the same spot on her head and remember our first meeting.

In the beginning was the Word. As creation was being birthed, Jesus was there to experience the special moment. He touched the first rays of light. He caressed Adam and Eve as they took humanity's first breaths. Jesus was there in the beginning, and he was also there at *your* beginning. He was present at the first creation, and now he is the pathway to a new creation.

Word spoke to the Hebrew-hearers of John's Gospel. So, too, the Greek speakers would readily recognize this term, but for different reasons.

The ancient Greeks loved their philosophy. A man named Heraclitus lived five centuries before Jesus, and he taught about the ever-changing world. In fact, he is the one who coined the phrase "You never step in the same river twice." Heraclitus also speculated that there exists a mysterious force stronger than chaos holding creation together. And the word Heraclitus used for this cosmic glue? You can probably guess it: The Word—the *logos*.[3]

John taps a word his Greek audience would easily grasp. In their own terms they would see a glimpse of Jesus's true identity. I even imagine a gasp or two as the Greek speakers read John's opening words for the first time. Even as our world seems in danger of spinning out of control, Jesus holds the chaos together with poise and ease.

To the Hebrews, *Word* points to creation.

To the Greeks, *Word* points to sustaining.

Both are true of Jesus!

Who is it that made us? And who holds our life and times in his steady hands? Who crafted us and who is it that cares for us through life come what may? It is Jesus. As it was in the beginning, so it is now, and so it will always be.

Creator.

Sustainer.

Word.

Jesus.

PLAIN WORDS

As a young parent, I found myself repeating the same five instructions to my children. "Pick up your room," "Say please," "Clean your plate," "Stop fighting," and "Didn't we ask you to go before we left the house?" We say such things because children require training. Said enough times, these instructions create habits, and habits form the character of a clean, polite, healthy, emotionally stable, and self-aware individual.

The fatherhood of God can be seen through this same lens. He, too, repeats one word, time and again, throughout the course of our lives. Are we in need of salvation? God speaks the name of Jesus. "There is salvation in no one else, for there is no other name under heaven given to people by which we must be saved," (Acts 4:12).

We are all given the privilege of choosing what personality we will develop. As we seek God in this matter, he says again the name of Jesus who serves as our model of personhood. "Adopt the same attitude as that of Christ Jesus," (Philippians 2:5).

When we are afraid, God again speaks the name of his son over our fears. "The LORD is my light and my salvation—whom should I fear?" (Psalm 27:1).

Even when we feel life is unfair, God yet again articulates the name of the One who faced his own fears as he faced down the cross.

> Let us run with endurance the race that lies before us, keeping our eyes on Jesus, the source and perfecter of our faith. For the joy that lay before him, he endured the cross, despising the shame, and sat down at the right hand of the throne of God.
>
> For consider him who endured such hostility from sinners against himself, so that you won't grow weary and give up.
>
> —Hebrews 12:1–3

The writer of Hebrews encourages us to keep our eyes on Jesus. He could just as easily have instructed us to keep our ears on Jesus.

The Eastern Orthodox tradition has the beautiful practice of the Jesus Prayer. Modeled after the words of the blind beggar in Jericho (Luke 18:35-43), the prayer in its most common form says, "Lord Jesus Christ, Son of God, have mercy on me."

For years, I have practiced this simple form of prayer. I find this prayer compelling because nearly half the prayer is spent on the name of Jesus. For me, this prayer has a calming and centering effect. Over time, the prayer has pruned itself down to a single word—Jesus. To pray his name is a privilege. The Jesus Prayer also reminds me that whatever else contends for my attention, my true need is nothing more and nothing less than Jesus himself.

If God is indeed speaking the name of his son, what does it say that we would echo the name of Jesus back to him? If nothing else, we agree with God that the source of our salvation, the formation of character, the facing of fear, and a selfless life lived in a self-centered world finds its ultimate expression in the name of Jesus.

PLAIN SPOKEN

If Jesus is our Creator and Sustainer and if his name reverberates through the cosmos and echoes into our souls, if Jesus is God's fullest and final Word to the human heart, what is our best response? The applications are likely endless, so I will suggest only four.

Passion

In recent days, I found myself bored with my job as a pastor. After twenty-five years of experience with nearly twenty of those years invested in the same church, I found myself moving absent-mindedly through the cycle of weddings, funerals, counseling, teaching, and crisis intervention. One week was blending into the next. No sooner was one Sunday checked off the calendar that another appeared on the horizon. I found myself thinking, "Here we go again." I felt in my bones the mantra of Ecclesiastes: "What has been is what will be, and what has been done is what will be done; there is nothing new under the sun," (Ecclesiastes 1:9).

Through the help of a good friend, I was able to see what I was lacking. My friend asked me, "If you could pastor any church on the planet, what would that church look like?" His question sparked within me a fresh vision, and with the vision came a fresh passion for how I am convinced God wants me to invest my life.

Someone might have demanded that I manufacture more passion

to address my sense of ministry fatigue. But such an endeavor would have proven a fruitless one. One can't simply conjure up passion and expect it to last. Deep, authentic passion is a by-product of greater vision.

Our passion for God works much the same way. If I were to prescribe greater passion for your relationship with God, I have no doubt that you would give it a good go. And you would very likely fail. Instead, as we catch a clearer vision of Jesus's full and true identity, greater passion for him will naturally follow.

Lisa Gherardini was born in 1479 in Florence, Italy. In her era, fifteen was considered a good age to marry. Custom also held that she should marry an older, well-established man. Lisa's husband was a thirty-year old silk merchant. Although Lisa did not bring money to the marriage, she was beautiful. By all accounts, her marriage was a happy one. Her husband loved her and she, in turn, genuinely respected him. To celebrate the birth of their second child, the husband hired an artist named Leonardo to paint Lisa's portrait.

Of course, Leonardo da Vinci's painting became known to us as the *Mona Lisa*. In 2005 a team of researchers confirmed the identity of the woman behind the world's most famous smile.[4] The project, called Discovering Mona Lisa, set out to discover all that could be learned about Lisa Gherardini. If you are willing to stand in line long enough, you can be one of six million people every year to behold her likeness in the Louvre. No doubt, Lisa's husband would be proud.

Might I suggest a similar project with Jesus? Let's set out to learn all we can about him. Learn about him from the pages of Scripture. He is in Genesis. Behold him in the Gospels. See him as he operates in the moments, days, and years of your life. He is with you in your car as you make your way to work, in your classroom as you take a test, and in your workplace as you make your living. He sits beside you as you eat breakfast and as you drift off to sleep. Jesus is present as I write these words, and he is present with you as you read them.

What passion will be ours as we discover Jesus where before we carelessly missed him! The adventure is afoot! Each of us can embark on a personal and lifelong project—Rediscovering Jesus Christ—if you will. Look for him, and passion will find its way to you.

Humility

The longer I live, the more I see humility as one of the most essential character qualities for Jesus-followers. The only time Jesus describes his own personality to his followers, he makes it clear that humility is the epicenter of his identity. ". . . I am lowly and humble in heart, and you will find rest for your souls," (Matthew 11:29).

Passion can easily lend itself to pride. If I become convinced that I have the inside scoop on appreciating God's presence, then I might view others of lesser insight as having lesser worth. Humility keeps passion in proper perspective. Jesus was magnificent, but he was also approachable.

I know very little about flowers. Only recently have I discovered flowers have a vocabulary all their own. Called fluorography, each species of flower communicates a unique emotion or message. Floral arrangements, then, not only communicate beauty to the eye, they also articulate messages to the heart. A red rose, of course, says, "I love you." The peony communicates, "I like you, but I am too shy to say so." The lily speaks to friendship. The tulip is a customary way of saying, "Welcome to your new home" or "Thank you for hosting." The carnation communicates, "You're fascinating, and I love you."[5]

It is the final flower and its intended message that I find most fitting. Look closely at the word. *Carnation*. Add just two letters to the beginning of this word and you have a term of great meaning to Christians: *In*-carnation.

Jesus's incarnation is the ultimate act of humility. Though God, he donned human flesh. In this way God communicates his fascination and love for us. If the one we call Lord is willing to embrace such humility, should not his followers?

Imagine what it means to embrace humility in a world that encourages pride. Instead of hating our enemies, we serve them. Instead of expecting others to pick up after us, we pick up after them. We recognize the small people because in Christ we know there are no small people.

The story is often retold of Muhammad Ali traveling aboard an airplane experiencing turbulence. The flight attendant, doing her job, asked Ali to buckle his seat belt. He exclaimed loud enough for others to hear, "Superman don't need no seat belt!" Without missing a beat the attendant shot back, "And Superman don't need no airplane!" Ali, who had a reputation for a good sense of humor, complied.[6]

None of us are Superman. There is only one. He is the Word. We are his servants. God forbid that we would see ourselves as superior to the One we have promised to serve.

Urgency

Just as humility balances the pride that passion can produce, so now urgency counters the passive tendencies of humility. Humility is not meant to make us the wallfollowers at the dance of life. When we hear the tune and feel the groove, we move to the dance floor whether anyone invites us or not. God is to be experienced now!

I must admit that on many days I am concerned about everything other than an urgent pursuit of God. This is the reason, as I have already mentioned, that I frequently make my way to a retreat spot not far from my home at Clear Creek Monastery. Several times a year, I enjoy the best of what Clear Creek has to offer: homemade Gouda cheese worth every calorie and, best of all, a sacred silence. The monks have purposefully eliminated every voice that threatens to drown out the Word. I emerge from Clear Creek having recalibrated the ears of my heart to the unique voice of Christ that tends to be lost amidst the noise of hasty living.

Each time I visit Clear Creek, I am confronted with a question: How radical am I willing to be in my pursuit of God? I do not believe all Christians should be monks. But all Christians are invited to listen to God's voice as he calls us to our own Spirit-led form of cutting-edge obedience. Instead of placidly accepting the status quo of my relationship with God, I am challenged to be intentional about curating a lifestyle that helps me best encounter God. This may mean eliminating some things such as excessive screen time or a toxic relationship or a long-held habit that hinders personal holiness. It may also mean adding some things to my daily life, disciplines that open my ears to the ever-speaking voice of God.

Reading the Bible is one such habit. Though simple, it is often neglected. When I read the Bible, I am familiarizing myself with God's manner of speaking.

Praying is another habit worth forming. Without it, I forget how to talk to and listen to the one person in the universe who understands me completely.

From one angle, this urgency toward intimacy with God demands a great deal of time. But from another angle, it requires no extra time at all. Brother Lawrence, a seventeenth-century monk, created the habit of being aware of God's presence both in the chapel at prayer and at the sink while washing dishes. Lawrence believed, rightly so, that God is always present. It is we who are typically absent.[7] Richness in life happens when we understand the availability of God's presence amidst the events that already fill our days. With this view of things, I may go about my life doing what I have always done; only now, the meaning of daily events is transformed because I am doing them with God My schedule looks the same as before. But now, any urgency I feel is not from the tasks I perform but from the presence of God I enjoy in each precious moment.

Wholehearted Surrender

My two sons have both managed to grow taller than me. Long past are the days that I could wrestle Caleb or Seth to the ground. Now, when we start our just-for-fun chest-bumping games of one-upmanship, my boys cock their chins skyward and position themselves inches away from my face, their eyes lock with mine in a slight downward angle. I respond to their attempt at physical intimidation with the words, "You may be bigger on the outside, but I am bigger on the inside." I remind them of the power I possess by virtue of being their father. I hold in my fatherly hands their ability to drive and date and go out with friends. I feel it is necessary occasionally (and jokingly) to remind my boys of their position in the family.

In much the same way, there are times I forget my place in reference to God. I seem pretty tall in my own eyes with a staff of people at work who report to me and a family at home who looks to me for provision and a church full of people who look to me for guidance. It is easy to convince myself that I am the one in charge. It is at such times that God speaks to me in subtle and not-so-subtle ways. The Word reminds me, "I am bigger than you—infinitely so." Jesus's life and sacrificial death and expectation-shattering resurrection remind me that he is infinite, and I am infinitesimal by comparison.

In the larger view of things, I am helpless. God is my provider. I depend on him for every good thing. The only fit response to this reality is a full-up, wholehearted surrender to him.

Jesus created us and sustains us. The words I have offered above scratch only the surface of the endless application of Jesus as our life's ultimate Word. Add to this list, if you like. As surely as Jesus is our God, he will serve as your guide.

THE LAST, LAST WORD

In 2012, England's Omega Auctions sold the personal Bible of Elvis Presley for $94,600. Throughout were handwritten notes from the king of rock 'n' roll himself. The next year, Einstein's signed Bible was sold for $68,500 at Bonhams in New York. Though a brilliant mind, Einstein himself claimed no religious convictions, at least publicly.[8]

How interesting that the value of a given Bible would be based on who happened to jot in its margins rather than who is revealed in its pages. The kings-of-whatever pale in comparison to the King of the universe. The most brilliant minds of science may miss what only the eyes of faith can see. To fixate on who owned a particular copy of Scripture is to miss the summoning voice of the One who wants to own us—heart, soul, future, and all.

The Word speaks on, articulating himself to anyone who has ears to hear.

Consider for a final time the words that have served to illuminate Scripture for us—*light*, *dust*, *breath*, *garden*, *river*, *eat*, *alone*, *naked*, *afraid*, and *sweat*. Behind each word remains the intimate presence of

Jesus. Beyond each term, Jesus reveals himself as that word's ultimate meaning. Above every word, both those on our list and the countless words of all human vernaculars, Jesus's name reigns eternal—a single-entry lexicon of true lordship. His name is language's highest use and grandest purpose. All other words bow before the singular and infinite Word that God longs to receive from every trembling tongue—the name of Jesus.

Speak, Lord, for your servants are listening.

TALK TO GOD

Lord God,
You spoke heavens and earth into being.
In an instant light and life became reality.
I, too, was summoned by name and gracefully given a purpose.

You speak again in Jesus.
New life and new light are mine to have!
When you speak my name, I am truly alive!
Amen.

TALK TO ONE ANOTHER

1. What are some moments or memories in your life when the name of Jesus has been particularly precious or powerful to you?

2. God reveals himself through his written word but also through the person of Jesus Christ. In what way is it uniquely valuable to see God personified?

3. Our first word was "Light" and our final word was "Jesus." Using the additional Scripture below, discuss how Jesus is the light of the world.

LISTEN TO SCRIPTURE

John 1:1–18
John 8:12
John 12:44–50

ACKNOWLEDGMENTS

To my children—Kira, Caleb, Seth. I enjoy watching each of you develop your own unique and independent relationship with our Lord. This is my greatest reward as your father. I love you, and I am proud of each of you.

To my church—First Baptist Tulsa. Thank you for the way you have loved my family and practiced patience with me for twenty years.

To the staff at First Baptist Tulsa—I am grateful to serve alongside each of you. Special thanks are in order to Chris Matthews for his help in developing the end-of-chapter questions, to Marissa Carter whose artistry in prayer serves me and this volume well, and to Brad Henderson for the generous use of his living room. And to my friends Jeff Elkins and Bobby Hart, it is an honor to serve the Lord shoulder to shoulder with you.

To my agents—Ann Spangler and Linda Kenny. Your fire for fresh thinking helped refine the level of creativity necessary for this volume.

And to the team at Worthy—Leeanna Nelson, whose shared passion for words and expert editorial hand pushed my writing to be its best. Jeana Ledbetter, you captured the essence of this book with a simple, abstract proposal; thank you for helping spread his Word across the kingdom. Jody Waldrup, who showed great patience as I agonized over cover art. Bart Dawson, thank you for using your gift of design to add style to my words and bring stories to life through typesetting this book. And to the sales, marketing, and publicity teams at Worthy and Hachette, your tireless efforts do not go unnoticed; I am indebted to you.

Finally, I am grateful for a man who took a chance on a twenty-nine-year-old kid to pastor a church in Tulsa, Oklahoma, two decades ago. Bob Jackson was always in my cheering section. He cheers on, only now among the great cloud of witnesses in heaven.

NOTES

ONE

1. "NASA Satellite Reveals How Much Saharan Feeds the Amazon's Plants," NASA.gov, February 22, 2015, https://www.nasa.gov/content/goddard/nasa-satellite-reveals-how-much-saharan-dust-feeds-amazon-s-plants.
2. John Lloyd, John Mitchinson, and James Harkin, *1227 Quite Interesting Facts to Blow Your Socks Off* (New York: W. W. Norton & Company, 2013), 272.
3. Lawrence O. Richards, *The Bible Reader's Companion* (Wheaton, IL: Chariot Victor Publishing, 1991), 329.
4. Richard Katula, *The Eloquence of Edward Everett: America's Greatest Orator* (New York: Peter Lang, 2010), 118.
5. Jacob Weisberg, "We are Hopelessly Hooked," *The New York Review of Books*, February 25, 2016, https://www.nybooks.com/articles/2016/02/25/we-are-hopelessly-hooked/.
6. K. Shryock Hood, *Once Upon a Time in a Dark and Scary Book: The Messages of Horror Literature for Children* (Jefferson, NC: McFarland & Company, 2018), 60.
7. Tanya Dean, *Theodor Geisel* (Philadelphia: Chelsea House Publishers, 2002), 78.

TWO

1. Phil Plait, "The Sky is Filled with Galaxies," *Slate*, October 14, 2016, https://slate.com/technology/2016/10/there-are-2-trillion-galaxies-in-the-universe.html.
2. Don Joseph Goewey, *The End of Stress: Four Steps to Rewire Your Brain* (New York: Atria, 2014), 153.
3. Walter W. Skeat, *The Concise Dictionary of English Etymology* (Hertfordshire, UK: Wordsworth editions, Ltd., 1993), 95.

4. John Walton, *Genesis: Zondervan Illustrated Bible Backgrounds Commentary* (Grand Rapids: Zondervan, 2009), 16.
5. John Stott, *The Radical Disciple: Some Neglected Aspects of Our Calling* (Downers Grove, IL: InterVarsity Press, 2010), 19–20.
6. Claire Cock-Starkey, "8 Surprising Facts About the Deepest Part of the Ocean," *Mental Floss,* January 16, 2017, http://mentalfloss.com/article/90796/8-surprising-facts-about-deepest-part-ocean.
7. Grant R. Osborne, Philip W. Comfort, and Wendell C. Hawley, *Cornerstone Biblical Commentary: The Gospel of John and 1-3 John,* Volume 13 (Carol Stream, IL: Tyndale House Publishers, 2007), 20.
8. Ben Myers, *The Apostles' Creed: A Guide to the Ancient Catechism* (Bellingham, WA; Lexham Press, 2018), 32.
9. John Ortberg, *Soul Keeping: Caring for the Most Important Part of You* (Grand Rapids, MI: Zondervan, 2014), 153.
10. David W. Givey, *The Social Thought of Thomas Merton: The Way of Nonviolence and Peace for the Future* (Winona, MN: Saint Mary's Press, 2009), xvii.
11. William Barclay, *The Gospel of John, Volume One* (Philadelphia: Westminster Press, 1956), 149.
12. Richard Rohr, *Falling Upward: A Spirituality for the Two Halves of Life* (San Francisco: Jossey-Bass, 2011), 118.
13. "About Us: Our Colorful Story," *Enchroma*, accessed March 2, 2019, https://enchroma.com/pages/about-us.

THREE

1. *The Book of Extraordinary Facts* (Morton Grove, IL: Publications International, Ltd., 2012), 94.
2. Paul Kalanithi, *When Breath Becomes Air* (New York: Random House, 2016), 131–132.
3. Walter W. Skeat, *The Concise Dictionary of English Etymology* (Hertfordshire, UK: Wordsworth editions, Ltd., 1993), 211.
4. Leonard Sweet, *Learn to Dance the Soul Salsa: 17 Surprising Steps for Godly Living in the 21st Century* (Grand Rapids, MI: Zondervan, 2000), 48.
5. Philip Yancey, *Prayer: Does It Make Any Difference?* (Grand Rapids, MI: Zondervan, 2006), 335.
6. Alan Cowell, "Michelangelo's David is Damaged," *The New York Times*;

September 15, 1991, https://www.nytimes.com/1991/09/15/world/michelangelo-s-david-is-damaged.html.

7. *The Book of Extraordinary Facts* (Morton Grove, IL: Publications International, Ltd., 2012), 332.
8. Denis Minns, *Irenaeus: An Introduction* (New York: T & T Clark, 2010), 146.
9. William Bryant Logan, *Dirt: The Ecstatic Skin of the Earth* (New York: W. W. Norton & Company, 1995), 17–19.
10. *Henry Wadsworth Longfellow: Poems and Other Writings*, ed. J. D. McClatchy (New York: Library of America, 2000), 3.

FOUR

1. Christine Hauser, "At 96, Dr. Heimlich Uses His Own Maneuver on Choking Victim," *The New York Times*; May 27, 2016, https://www.nytimes.com/2016/05/28/us/dr-heimlich-uses-his-own-maneuver-on-choking-victim.html.
2. *Holman Bible Dictionary*, ed. Trent C. Butler (Nashville: Holman Bible Publishers, 1991), 1299.
3. John Walton, *Genesis: Zondervan Illustrated Bible Backgrounds Commentary* (Grand Rapids, MI: Zondervan, 2009), 26.
4. Walter W. Skeat, *The Concise Dictionary of English Etymology* (Hertfordshire, UK: Wordsworth editions, Ltd., 1993), 458–459.
5. "Today is the birthday," The Writer's Almanac with Garrison Keillor, accessed March 2, 2019, https://www.writersalmanac.org/index.html%3Fp-10428.html.
6. Michael Casey, *Strangers to the City: Reflections on the Beliefs and Values of the Rule of Saint Benedict* (Brewster, MA: Paraclete Press, 2008), 89–90.
7. C. S. Lewis, *The Lion, the Witch and the Wardrobe* (New York: Macmillan Publishing Company, 1950), 164.
8. Lewis, *The Lion, the Witch and the Wardrobe*, 166.
9. "Breathe on Me," *Digital Songs & Hymns*, accessed March 2, 2019, http://www.digitalsongsandhymns. com /songs/3922.
10. Doris Kearns Goodwin, *Leadership: In Turbulent Times* (New York: Simon & Schuster, 2018), 24.
11. G. K. Chesterton, *The Collected Works of G. K. Chesterton: Volume. X: Collected Poetry, Part I* (San Francisco: Ignatius Press, 1994) 43.

FIVE

1. *The Book of Extraordinary Facts* (Morton Grove, IL: Publications International, Ltd., 2012), 332.
2. John Walton, *The Lost World of Adam and Eve* (Downers Grove, IL: InterVarsity Press, 2015), 48.
3. Victor Kuligin, *The Language of Salvation: Discovering the Riches of What It Means to Be Saved* (Bellingham, WA: Lexham Press, 2015), 172.
4. Joyce Kilmer, *Poems, Essays and Letters in Two Volumes, Volume 1: Memoir and Poems* (New York: George H. Doran Company, 1918), 180.

SIX

1. Derek Kidner, *Genesis: Tyndale Old Testament Commentaries* (Downers Grove, IL: Inter-Varsity Press, 1967), 64.
2. Dan Lewis, *Now I Know: The Revealing Stories Behind the World's Most Interesting Facts* (Avon, MA: Adams Media, 2013), 116–117.
3. Shirley Carter Hughson, *The Spiritual Letters of Father Hughson O.H.C.* (West Park, NY: Holy Cross Press, 1953), 96.
4. Donald Whitney, *Ten Questions to Diagnose Your Spiritual Health* (Colorado Springs, CO: NavPress, 2001), 17–23.
5. "World's Oldest Living Animal, 184-Year-Old Tortoise Named Jonathan, Has First Ever Bath," *The Telegraph,* March 23, 2016, https://www.telegraph.co.uk/good-news/2016/03/23/ worlds-oldest-living-animal-aged-184-has-first-ever-bath/.
6. Carl Sagan, *Murmurs of Earth: The Voyager Interstellar Record* (New York: Random House, 1978), 194.

SEVEN

1. "Deep Blue Defeats Garry Kasparov in Chess Match," History.com, August 21, 2018, https://www.history.com/this-day-in-history/deep-blue-defeats-garry-kasparov-in-chess-match.
2. Weston Williams, "What Makes a Knot Strong? Scientists Have Figured Out How Your Shoelaces Untie Themselves," *The Christian Science Monitor*, April 12, 2017, https://www. csmonitor.com/Science/2017/0412/What-makes-a-knot-strong-Scientists-have-figured-out-how-your-shoelaces-untie-themselves.

3. Charles H. Spurgeon, *Evening by Evening: A New Edition of the Classic Devotional Based on the Holy Bible, English Standard Version*, ed. Alistair Begg (Wheaton, IL: Crossway, 2007), 339.

EIGHT

1. "The Epidemic of Lonliness," *The Week*, January 6, 2019, https://theweek.com/articles/815518/ epidemic-loneliness.
2. *The Book of Extraordinary Facts* (Morton Grove, IL: Publications International, Ltd., 2012), 604.
3. Cited in Peter J. Leithart, *Traces of the Trinity: Signs of God in Creation and Human Experience* (Grand Rapids, MI: Brazos, 2015), 17.
4. Jacob Weisberg, "We are Hopelessly Hooked," *The New York Review of Books*, February 25, 2016, https://www.nybooks.com/articles/2016/02/25/we-are-hopelessly-hooked/.
5. Henri J. M. Nouwen, *The Only Necessary Thing: Living a Prayerful Life*, ed. Wendy Wilson Greer (New York: The Crossroad Publishing Company, 2015), 153.
6. Emilie Griffin, *Small Surrenders: A Lenten Journey* (Brewster, MA: Paraclete Press, 2007), 48.
7. Dan Lewis, *Now I Know More: The Revealing Stories Behind Even More of the World's Most Interesting Facts* (Avon, MA: Adams Media, 2014), 216–217.

NINE

1. Christopher Green, *Picasso: Architecture and Vertigo* (New Haven, CT: Yale University Press, 2005), 75–78.
2. Søren Kierkegaard, *Papers and Journals: A Selection* (New York: Penguin Books, 1996), 295.
3. John Walton, *Genesis: Zondervan Illustrated Bible Backgrounds Commentary* (Grand Rapids, MI: Zondervan, 2009), 35.
4. Francis Thompson, *The Hound of Heaven* (New York: Dodd, Mead and Company, 1930), 45–60.
5. Rankin Wilbourne, *Union with Christ: The Way to Know and Enjoy God* (Colorado Springs, CO: David C Cook, 2016), 58.
6. *The Book of Extraordinary Facts* (Morton Grove, IL: Publications International, Ltd., 2012), 604–605.

TEN

1. William Bryant Logan, *Dirt: The Ecstatic Skin of the Earth* (New York: W. W. Norton & Company, 1995), 186.
2. Richard L. Pratt, Jr., *He Gave Us Stories: The Bible Student's Guide to Interpreting Old Testament Narratives* (Phillipsburg, NJ: P & R Publishing, 1990), 87.
3 Henri J. M. Nouwen, *The Only Necessary Thing: Living a Prayerful Life*, ed. Wendy Wilson Greer (New York: The Crossroad Publishing Company, 2015), 195–196.
4. Dorene Internicola, "Oldest Female Bodybuilder Loves Pumping Iron," *Reuters*; May 28, 2012, https://torontosun.com/2012/05/28/oldest-female-bodybuilder-loves-pumping-iron/wcm/3b0852eb-d097-4d27-b496-6a363e15a5bd.
5. "About," Barbara Hillary, accessed May 3, 2019, https://barbarahillary.com/about/.
6. Anna Green, "The First Woman to Hike the Appalachian Trial Was 67 Years Old," *Mental Floss*; October 26, 2015, http://mentalfloss.com/article/70374/first-woman-hike-appalachian-trail-was-67-years-old.

ELEVEN

1. Laura Donnelly, "Your Life Really Does Flash Before Your Eyes Before You Die, Study Suggests," *The Daily Telegraph*, January 29, 2017, https://www.telegraph.co.uk/news/2017/ 01/29/life-really-does-flash-eyes-die-study-suggests/.
2. John Walton, *Genesis: Zondervan Illustrated Bible Backgrounds Commentary* (Grand Rapid, MI: Zondervan, 2009), 27.
3. *The Book of Extraordinary Facts* (Morton Grove, IL: Publications International, Ltd., 2012), 342.
4. Edwin H. Friedman, *A Failure of Nerve: Leadership in the Age of the Quick Fix* (New York: Church Publishing, 2017), 204.
5. Sol Stein, *Stein on Writing: A Master Editor of Some of the Most Successful Writers of Our Century Shares His Craft Techniques and Strategies* (New York: St. Martin's Press, 1995), 12–13.
6. *Churchill By Himself: The Definitive Collection of Quotations*, ed. Richard Langworth (New York: PublicAffairs, 2008), 580.

7. William D. Edwards, "On the Physical Death of Jesus Christ," *JAMA,* Volume 255, no. 11 (1986): 1455-1463, http://jama.jamanetwork.com/article.aspx?articleid=403315.
8. *The Handy Science Answer Book: Compiled by the Science and Technology Department of the Carnegie Library of Pittsburg,* compiled by the Carnegie Library of Pittsburg, eds. James E. Bobick and Naomi E. Balaban (Detroit, MI: Visible Ink Press, 2011), 232.
9. Shaunacy Ferro, "The 392-Year-Old Bonsai That Survived Hiroshima," *Mental Floss,* February 4, 2017, http://mentalfloss.com/article/91799/392-year-old-bonsai-survived-hiroshima.

TWELVE

1. *Bartlett's Book of Anecdotes,* eds. Clifton Fadiman and Andre Bernard (Boston, MA: Little, Brown and Company, 2000), 104.
2. Frederick Buechner, *A Room Called Remember: Uncollected Pieces* (San Francisco: HarperCollins, 1992), 83.
3. William Barclay, *Good Tidings of Great Joy: The Birth of Jesus the Messiah* (Louisville, KY: Westminster John Knox Press, 1999), 9–10.
4. Dianne Hales, *Mona Lisa: A Life Discovered* (New York: Simon & Schuster, 2014).
5. *The Book of Extraordinary Facts* (Morton Grove, IL: Publications International, Ltd., 2012), 188.
6. John Dickson, *Humilitas: A Lost Key to Life, Love, and Leadership* (Grand Rapids, MI: Zondervan, 2011), 56–57.
7. Without reservation, I recommend reading *The Practice of the Presence of God* by Brother Lawrence. A more modern take on the same spiritual discipline is found in Frank Laubach's *Letters by a Modern Mystic.*
8. Kenneth A. Briggs, *The Invisible Bestseller: Searching for the Bible in America* (Grand Rapids, MI: Eerdmans, 2016), 9–10.

ABOUT THE AUTHOR

DERON SPOO is the pastor of First Baptist Church in Tulsa, Oklahoma. For the past two decades, Deron has guided the church as it transitioned from being simply a downtown church to a regional church committed to urban ministry. Church members describe him as "down to earth" and "authentic." His television devotionals, *First Things First*, reach 100,000 people each week. Deron is a graduate of Southwestern Baptist Theological Seminary. He is the author of *The Good Book: 40 Chapters That Reveal the Bible's Biggest Ideas* released by David C Cook in 2017. He and his wife, Paula, have three children.